EVERY DAY COUNTS®

PRACTICE COUNTS

Patsy F. Kanter • Janet G. Gillespie • Andy Clark

GRADE
4

GReaT SouRCe®
EDUCATION GROUP
A Houghton Mifflin Company
New Ways to Know℠

Credits

Cover Design: Susan Havice
Cover Illustration: Rob Dunlavey
Layout Production: Taurins Design Associates

Printed in the United States of America

Great Source® and *Every Day Counts*® are registered trademarks of Houghton Mifflin Company.

International Standard Book Number: 0–669–46929–7

1 2 3 4 5 6 7 8 9 10   POO   05 04 03 02 01 00 99

URL address: http://www.greatsource.com/

DAY 1

Look at the ten grids. Then fill in the blanks.

1. $6 + 6 =$ _____ so $12 - 6 =$ _____

2. $6 + 7 =$ _____ so $13 - 6 =$ _____

3. $5 + 5 =$ _____ so $10 - 5 =$ _____

4. $5 + 6 =$ _____ so $11 - 5 =$ _____

5. $7 + 7 =$ _____ so $14 - 7 =$ _____

6. $7 + 8 =$ _____ so $15 - 7 =$ _____

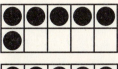

Draw a line under each even number.

7. 1 2 3 4 5 6 7 8 9 10 11 12

DAY 2

Look at the ten grids. Then fill in the blanks.

1. $8 + 8 =$ _____ so $16 - 8 =$ _____

2. $8 + 9 =$ _____ so $17 - 8 =$ _____

3. $7 + 7 =$ _____ so $14 - 7 =$ _____

4. $7 + 8 =$ _____ so $15 - 7 =$ _____

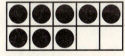

Tell how much money is shown here.

5. _____

6. _____

7. _____

8. _____

9.  _____

DAY 3

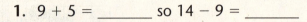

Look at the ten grids. Then fill in the blanks.

1. 9 + 5 = _____ so 14 − 9 = _____

2. 9 + 7 = _____ so 16 − 9 = _____

3. 9 + 9 = _____ so 18 − 9 = _____

4. 9 + 4 = _____ so 13 − 9 = _____

5. 9 + 6 = _____ so 15 − 9 = _____

6. 9 + 8 = _____ so 17 − 9 = _____

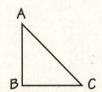

7. Name two things that are alike about these figures. _____

_____

8. Name two things that are different about these figures. _____

_____

DAY 4

Look at the ten grids. Then fill in the blanks.

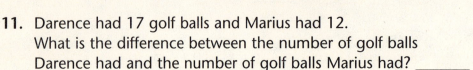

1. 8 + 1 = _____   2. 8 + 2 = _____

3. 8 + 3 = _____   4. 8 + 4 = _____

5. 8 + 5 = _____   6. 8 + 6 = _____

7. 8 + 7 = _____   8. 8 + 8 = _____

9. 8 + 9 = _____   10. 8 + 10 = _____

11. Darence had 17 golf balls and Marius had 12.
    What is the difference between the number of golf balls
    Darence had and the number of golf balls Marius had? _____

Dᴀy 5

Look at the ten grids. Then fill in the blanks.

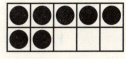

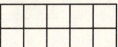

1. 7 + 4 = _____ so 11 − 7 = _____ or 11 − 4 = _____

2. 7 + 5 = _____ so _____ or _____

3. 7 + 6 = _____ so _____ or _____

4. 7 + 8 = _____ so _____ or _____

5. What strategy did you use to find the missing number? _____

   _____

   _____

6. The class went on a field trip. They split into two groups. One group had 8 boys and 5 girls. The other group had 6 girls and 8 boys. How many children were in the class? _____

7. How many boys and how many girls were there? _____

8. Imagine that the number of children in the class was 28. Think of 3 ways the teacher might have divided the students into 2 groups.

   _____

   _____

Dᴀy 6

Write the missing addend.

1. 2 + 2 + 2 + 2 + _____ = 10   2. 2 + 2 + 3 + _____ = 10

3. 5 + 5 + _____ = 15   4. 2 + 3 + 5 + _____ = 15

Continue these patterns.

5. 0, 2, 4, 6, _____, 18

6. 0, 3, 6, 9, _____, 27

DAY 7

Write the missing addend.

1. 3 + _____ + 3 + 3 + 3 = 15

2. 2 + 3 + 2 + 3 + _____ = 15

3. 5 + 3 + 2 + _____ = 20

4. 5 + 5 + 3 + 3 + 2 + _____ = 20

5. 10 + 5 + _____ + 5 = 30

6. 2 + 3 + _____ + 5 + 10 = 30

Draw the hands on these clocks to show the correct time.

7. 10:07 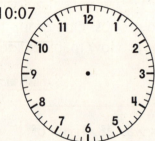   8. 10:29 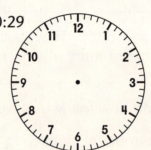   9. 10:48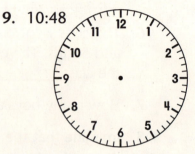

DAY 8

Complete the number sentence.

1. 2 + 2 + 3 + 5 = 10 + _____

2. 5 + 5 + 5 + 5 = 10 + _____

3. 3 + 3 + 3 + 3 + 3 = 5 + _____ + 5

4. 10 + 3 + 2 + 10 = _____ + 10 + 10

5. 2 + 3 + _____ + 2 = 3 + 3 + 3 + 3

6. _____ + 5 + 3 + 2 = 5 + 5 + 10

Use the geoboard to solve the problem.

7. How many squares can you make? _____

•   •   •   •

•   •   •   •

•   •   •   •

•   •   •   •

DAY 9

Compare. Write < (is less than) or > (is greater than).

1. 10 _____ 2 + 2 + 2
2. 20 _____ 10 + 10 + 10
3. 5 + 5 + 5 _____ 20
4. 2 + 2 + 2 + 2 + 2 _____ 15

5. Pretend you have $25 in your bank account today. How much money will be in your account if you deposit $5 each week for the next 3 weeks? _____

6. How much money will be in your account if you take out $5 each week for the next 3 weeks? _____

DAY 10   CHECKPOINT

Look at the ten grids. Then fill in the blanks.

1. 9 + _____ = 18
2. 9 + _____ = 17
3. 9 + _____ = 16
4. 9 + _____ = 15
5. 9 + _____ = 14
6. 9 + _____ = 13

Compare. Write < (is less than) or > (is greater than).

7. 3 + 2 + 5 + 10 _____ 5 + 3 + 2
8. 10 + 5 + 5 _____ 3 + 2 + 5 + 5
9. 10 + 10 + 2 + 2 _____ 2 + 3 + 10 + 10
10. 3 + 3 + 3 + 2 + 2 _____ 5 + 5 + 2

11. How can you make $0.37 with the fewest coins? _____

_____

12. What time is on the clock? _____

DAY 11

Add.

1.	2.	3.	4.	5.
5	6	8	9	10
⑥	⑦	⑨	⑩	⑪
+ 7	+ 8	+ 10	+ 11	+ 12

6. What is the relationship between the circled number and the sum in problems 1 through 5? _____

_____

_____

Continue these patterns.

7. 1, 3, 5, 7, 9, _____, 21

8. 1, 4, 7, 10, 13, _____, 28.

DAY 12

Add.

1.	2.	3.	4.	5.
17	18	20	21	22
⑱	⑲	㉑	㉒	㉓
+ 19	+ 20	+ 22	+ 23	+ 24

6. What is the relationship between the circled number and the sum in problems 1 through 5? _____

_____

_____

A yard equals 3 feet. Use this information to fill in the blanks.

7. 2 yards = _____

8. 3 yards = _____

9. 5 yards = _____

DAY 13

Add.

1.	2.	3.	4.	5.
11	13	15	17	19
(13)	(15)	(17)	(19)	(21)
+ 15	+ 17	+ 19	+ 21	+ 23

6. What is the relationship between the circled number and the sum in problems

1 through 5? _____

_____

_____

Use the geoboard to solve the problem.

7. Explain why you think it is possible to make more

than 15 different triangles on this geoboard.

_____

_____

DAY 14

Add mentally.

1.	2.	3.	4.	5.
10	12	14	16	18
12	14	16	18	20
+ 14	+ 16	+ 18	+ 20	+ 22

6. How did you solve problem 3? _____

_____

7. Sarah collects sports cards. She has 78.
James also collects sports cards. He has 39.
How many sports cards do they have all together? _____

8. What is the difference between the
number James has and the number Sarah has? _____

DAY 15

Fill in the number in the circle.

1. 11	**2.** 18	**3.** 15	**4.** 28	**5.** 5
◯	◯	◯	◯	◯
+ 13	+ 22	+ 19	+ 30	+ 15
36	60	51	87	30

6. Renaldo wants to buy 2 snacks from the vending machine. One costs $0.80 and one costs $0.65. Renaldo only has 6 quarters. The machine makes change. Tell what coins Renaldo might use to buy each treat. _____

_____

_____

DAY 16

Write the + or − in the blank.

1. 13 = 6 _____ 7   **2.** 10 _____ 4 = 6   **3.** 9 _____ 2 = 11

4. 7 _____ 5 = 12   **5.** 9 = 16 _____ 7   **6.** 68 + 27 = 27 _____ 68

Subtract. Look for a pattern.

7.	**8.**	**9.**	**10.**
22	24	26	28
− 2	− 2	− 2	− 2

11.	**12.**	**13.**	**14.**
23	25	27	29
− 2	− 2	− 2	− 2

15. In problems 7 through 10, the differences are even. In problems 11 through 14, the differences are odd. Why do you think this is so? _____

_____

_____

DAY 17

Add.

1.	338 + 338	**2.**	363 + 363	**3.**	366 + 366	**4.**	388 + 388
5.	633 + 633	**6.**	636 + 636	**7.**	838 + 838	**8.**	833 + 833

There are 100 centimeters in a meter. Use this fact to fill in the blanks.

9. 2 meters = _____ centimeters

10. 3 meters = _____

11. 4 meters = _____

DAY 18

Subtract.

1.	866 − 433	**2.**	868 − 434	**3.**	648 − 324	**4.**	684 − 342
5.	468 − 234	**6.**	486 − 243	**7.**	846 − 423	**8.**	848 − 424

9. Think about a circle and a rectangle. How is a circle different from a rectangle

or a triangle? _____

_____

_____

DAY 19

Subtract.

1.	897 − 543	2.	879 − 534	3.	877 − 533	4.	899 − 544
5.	987 − 453	6.	978 − 435	7.	977 − 433	8.	988 − 455

9. Regina went to the store. She bought 16 orange drinks in cans,
17 cherry drinks in boxes and 18 grape drinks in bottles.
How many drinks did she buy? _____

DAY 20

Subtract.

1.	987 − 635	2.	978 − 653	3.	977 − 655	4.	988 − 633
5.	897 − 365	6.	879 − 356	7.	899 − 366	8.	877 − 355

9. These are the boys and girls in Mrs. Garcia's math group.

Dimitri	**Alicia**
Paul	**Elizabeth**
Mateo	**Angela**
Andy	**Lynnie**

Mrs. Garcia likes one boy and one girl to work together for math partner games.

List three different ways she can group them. _____

_____

_____

MONTHLY ASSESSMENT

1. Color in a pattern that is ABAB and put a yellow star on every fifth day. Start the pattern on the first Sunday in the month.

Sunday	Monday	Tuesday	Wednesday	Thursday	Friday	Saturday

2. Write three statements about what you see on your calendar pattern.

_____

_____

_____

_____

_____

_____

_____

MONTHLY ASSESSMENT

Fill in the blanks.

1. 18 − _____ = 9
2. 8 + _____ = 13
3. _____ − 8 = 9
4. _____ + 6 = 14
5. 14 − _____ = 7
6. 7 + _____ = 13
7. 13 − _____ = 7
8. 8 + 9 = _____
9. 14 − 8 = _____
10. 7 + _____ = 14
11. _____ − 5 = 8
12. 9 + _____ = 18
13. _____ × 2 = 18
14. _____ × 2 = 8
15. 6 × _____ = 12
16. 3 × _____ = 6
17. 8 × 2 = _____
18. 7 × 2 = _____
19. _____ × 2 = 10
20. _____ × 2 = 4
21. 5 + _____ + 2 + 3 = 20
22. 10 + 2 + _____ = 15
23. 10 + 5 + _____ + 2 = 2 + 3 + 5 + 10
24. _____ × 2 = 10 + 4
25. 5 × _____ = 10 + 10
26. 6 × 2 = 10 + _____

Add mentally.

27.	28.	29.	30.	31.
8	12	18	20	13
10	14	19	19	11
+ 12	+ 16	+ 20	+ 18	+ 10

Subtract mentally.

32.	33.	34.	35.	36.
866	222	644	648	424
− 433	− 111	− 322	− 324	− 212

MONTHLY ASSESSMENT

A vending machine takes coins or bills. A can of soda costs $0.65.
A candy bar costs $0.60. A package of gum costs $0.55. A package
of cookies costs $0.70.

1. If you have 2 quarters, 1 dime,
   and a penny, which items can you buy? _____

2. If you put a dollar bill into the machine
   and buy a soda, how much change will you get? _____

3. If you have 2 one-dollar bills and you buy candy
   and gum, how much money will you have left? _____

4. You have these coins and the machine is out

   of change. What coins would you use to buy

   gum, then a soda? _____

   _____

   _____

**Get these counters, or write their colors on squares
of paper. Put them in a paper bag.**

⚪⚪⚪ Red   🔵🔵🔵 Blue   ⚫⚫⚫ Green

5. Predict which counter would be picked most often if
   you picked one from the bag, then put it back, 10 times. _____

6. Pick a counter from the bag. Record it in the table with
   a tally. Pick and record 4 more times. Do you want to
   change your prediction? If you do, explain why.

Red	Blue	Green

   _____

7. Pick and record 20 more times. Would you describe the
   colors as *equally likely* or *not equally likely* to be picked? Explain.

   _____

   _____

   _____

MONTHLY ASSESSMENT

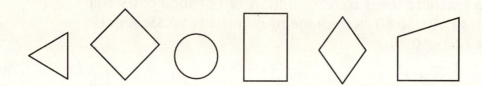

1. Name any 3 of these figures. _____

   _____

2. Tell 2 ways your figures are alike. _____

   _____

   _____

3. Tell 2 ways your figures are different. _____

   _____

   _____

4. Name another shape. _____

5. Describe how the figure in problem 4 is alike or different
   from the figures in problem 1.

   _____

   _____

There are 100 centimeters in a meter. Use this fact to fill in the blanks.

6. 200 centimeters = _____ meters

7. 300 centimeters = _____

8. 5 meters = _____

9. 10 meters = _____

There are 3 feet in a yard. Use this fact to fill in the blanks.

10. 6 feet = _____ yards

11. 30 feet = _____

12. 6 yards = _____ feet

13. 10 yards = _____

Multiply.

1. $2 \times 2 =$ _____
2. $4 \times 2 =$ _____
3. $8 \times 2 =$ _____

4. $3 \times 2 =$ _____
5. $6 \times 2 =$ _____
6. $9 \times 2 =$ _____

7. $1 \times 2 =$ _____
8. $7 \times 2 =$ _____
9. $10 \times 2 =$ _____

10. Continue the pattern.

____ ____ ____ ____ ____

DAY 2 ·

Multiply.

1. $2 \times 2 =$ _____ (Double it, or $\times$ 2) $=$ _____ (Double it, or $\times$ 2) $=$ _____ (Double it, or $\times$ 2) $=$ _____

2. $3 \times 2 =$ _____ (Double it, or $\times$ 2) $=$ _____ (Double it, or $\times$ 2) $=$ _____ (Double it, or $\times$ 2) $=$ _____

3. $4 \times 2 =$ _____ (Double it, or $\times$ 2) $=$ _____ (Double it, or $\times$ 2) $=$ _____ (Double it, or $\times$ 2) $=$ _____

4. Give three different ways to make 25 cents using pennies, nickels, and dimes.

_____ pennies   _____ pennies   _____ pennies

_____ nickels   _____ nickels   _____ nickels

_____ dimes   _____ dimes   _____ dimes

25 cents   **25** cents   **25** cents

DAY 3

Multiply.

1. $2 \times 3 = $ _____

2. $4 \times 3 = $ _____

3. $8 \times 3 = $ _____

4. $3 \times 3 = $ _____

5. $6 \times 3 = $ _____

6. $9 \times 3 = $ _____

7. $1 \times 3 = $ _____

8. $7 \times 3 = $ _____

9. $10 \times 3 = $ _____

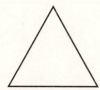 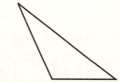

10. Name 2 attributes that are the same about these two-dimensional figures.

   _____

11. Name 2 attributes that are different about these figures. _____

   _____

DAY 4

Add. Then add the sums.

1. $1 + 1 = $ _____

2. $2 + 2 = $ _____

3. $3 + 3 = $ _____

4. $4 + 4 = $ _____

5. $5 + 5 = $ _____

6. Total $= $ _____

7. What is the pattern in the sums?

   _____

   _____

   _____

   _____

   _____

8. Sheryl Sum and Patsy Product are collecting money for a holiday party. Sheryl collected $10.00 the first week and doubled it the second week. Patsy collected $11.00 the first week and doubled it the second week. How much have Sheryl and Patsy collected all together after the first two weeks? _____

DAY 5

Multiply.

1. $2 \times 5 =$ _____
2. $4 \times 5 =$ _____
3. $8 \times 5 =$ _____
4. $3 \times 5 =$ _____
5. $6 \times 5 =$ _____
6. $9 \times 5 =$ _____
7. $1 \times 5 =$ _____
8. $7 \times 5 =$ _____
9. $10 \times 5 =$ _____

Paul Plus used beans to show the division of each number from 1 to 16 into groups of three. Maya Minus recorded the results. She said, "I see a pattern in the remainders. They go 1, 2, 0 and keep repeating."

Fill in the blanks by predicting the answers through 16.

10. $1 \div 3 = 0 \text{ R1}$ $5 \div 3 = 1 \text{ R2}$ $9 \div 3 =$ _____ $13 \div 3 =$ _____
11. $2 \div 3 = 0 \text{ R2}$ $6 \div 3 = 2 \text{ R0}$ $10 \div 3 =$ _____ $14 \div 3 =$ _____
12. $3 \div 3 = 1 \text{ R0}$ $7 \div 3 = 2 \text{ R1}$ $11 \div 3 =$ _____ $15 \div 3 =$ _____
13. $4 \div 3 = 1 \text{ R1}$ $8 \div 3 =$ _____ $12 \div 3 =$ _____ $16 \div 3 =$ _____

14. Do you agree with what Maya said? _____

15. Why or why not? _____

_____

DAY 6

Find the missing numbers.

1. $2 \times$ _____ $= 10$
2. $3 \times 5 =$ _____
3. $9 \times$ _____ $= 18$
4. _____ $\times 2 = 8$
5. $6 \times$ _____ $= 12$
6. $7 \times 5 =$ _____
7. $6 \times 5 =$ _____
8. $9 \times 5 =$ _____
9. $8 \times$ _____ $= 40$

10. Continue the pattern.

Try this.

11. What would be the next piece? _____

DAY 7

Divide.

1. $21 \div \underline{\hspace{1.5cm}} = 7$ 2. $30 \div 3 = \underline{\hspace{1.5cm}}$

3. $24 \div \underline{\hspace{1.5cm}} = 3$ 4. $6 \div 2 = \underline{\hspace{1.5cm}}$

5. $18 \div \underline{\hspace{1.5cm}} = 3$ 6. $9 \div 3 = \underline{\hspace{1.5cm}}$

7. $27 \div 9 = \underline{\hspace{1.5cm}}$ 8. $12 \div 4 = \underline{\hspace{1.5cm}}$

9. $3 \div \underline{\hspace{1.5cm}} = 3$ 10. $15 \div 5 = \underline{\hspace{1.5cm}}$

11. Lila says it is quarter to eight and

    Hari says it is 7:45. Who is right? _____

12. Explain your thinking. _____

_____

DAY 8

1. $5 \div \underline{\hspace{1.5cm}} = 2 \text{ R}1$ 2. $15 \div 2 = \underline{\hspace{1.5cm}}$

3. $7 \div 2 = \underline{\hspace{1.5cm}}$ 4. $17 \div 2 = \underline{\hspace{1.5cm}}$

5. $9 \div 2 = \underline{\hspace{1.5cm}}$ 6. $19 \div 2 = \underline{\hspace{1.5cm}}$

7. What pattern do you see with these division problems? _____

_____

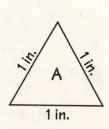
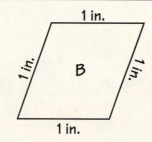
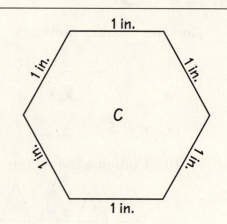

_____   _____   _____

8. Compare these figures. Write the name under each shape.

9. How many of figure A would fit into figure B? _____

10. How many of figure A would fit into figure C? _____

DAY 9

Fill in the blanks.

1. $17 \div 3 = \underline{\hspace{2cm}}$ R $\underline{\hspace{1cm}}$
2. $(3 \times \underline{\hspace{1.5cm}}) + 2 = 17$
3. $15 \div 2 = \underline{\hspace{2cm}}$ R $\underline{\hspace{1cm}}$
4. $(2 \times \underline{\hspace{1.5cm}}) + 1 = 15$
5. $19 \div 3 = \underline{\hspace{2cm}}$ R $\underline{\hspace{1cm}}$
6. $(3 \times \underline{\hspace{1.5cm}}) + 1 = 19$
7. $18 \div 2 = \underline{\hspace{2cm}}$ R $\underline{\hspace{1cm}}$
8. $(2 \times \underline{\hspace{1.5cm}}) + 0 = 18$

9. Aly is thinking of a number and here is what she says:
   My number divided by 1 has no remainder
   My number divided by 2 has no remainder
   My number divided by 5 has no remainder.
   My number is less than 20. What is my number? $\underline{\hspace{2cm}}$

DAY 10   CHECKPOINT

Fill in the blanks.

1. $\underline{\hspace{1.5cm}} \times 2 = 8$
2. $6 \times \underline{\hspace{1.5cm}} = 12$
3. $7 \times 5 = \underline{\hspace{1.5cm}}$
4. $6 \times 5 = \underline{\hspace{1.5cm}}$
5. $3 \times \underline{\hspace{1.5cm}} = 21$
6. $1 \times 2 = \underline{\hspace{1.5cm}}$
7. $24 \div \underline{\hspace{1.5cm}} = 3$
8. $6 \div 2 = \underline{\hspace{1.5cm}}$
9. $5 \div \underline{\hspace{1.5cm}} = 2$ R1
10. $15 \div 2 = \underline{\hspace{1.5cm}}$
11. $19 \div 3 = \underline{\hspace{1.5cm}}$
12. $(3 \times \underline{\hspace{1.5cm}}) + 1 = 19$

13. How many of these triangles will
    fit inside the square? Explain.

    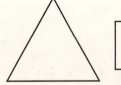

    $\underline{\hspace{6cm}}$

14. The clock shows 12:15. Tell two ways to say what time it is.

    $\underline{\hspace{14cm}}$

    $\underline{\hspace{14cm}}$

Tell how much money is shown here.

15.  $\underline{\hspace{2cm}}$

16.  $\underline{\hspace{2cm}}$

DAY 11

Fill in the blanks.

1. 15 + 15 = _____	2. 16 + 16 = _____	3. 17 + 17 = _____
15 + 16 = _____	16 + 17 = _____	17 + 18 = _____
30 − 15 = _____	32 − 16 = _____	34 − 17 = _____
31 − 15 = _____	33 − 16 = _____	35 − 17 = _____
31 − 16 = _____	33 − 17 = _____	35 − 18 = _____

Continue these patterns.

4. 1, 4, 5, 8, 9, 12, _____, 21.

5. 1, 3, 6, 10, 15, _____, 55.

DAY 12

Subtract.

1. 45 − 20 = _____

2. 46 − 21 = _____

3. 47 − 22 = _____

4. 48 − 23 = _____

5. 49 − 24 = _____

6. What pattern do you see in the answers? _____

_____

_____

7. Use quarters, dimes, nickels, and pennies. List three different ways to make 36 cents.

_____

_____

_____

DAY 13

Solve mentally.

1. 49 + _____ = 82   2. 38 + _____ = 82

   49 + _____ = 75   38 + _____ = 75

   49 + _____ = 63   38 + _____ = 63

   49 + _____ = 55   38 + _____ = 55

3. How did you get your answers? _____

   _____

 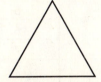

4. Draw a line of symmetry through each figure.

5. How do you know it is a line of symmetry? _____

   _____

   _____

   _____

DAY 14

Solve mentally.

1. 37 + _____ = 90   2. _____ − 27 = 33

   38 + _____ = 90   _____ − 28 = 22

   39 + _____ = 90   _____ − 29 = 11

3. Anita is doubling a recipe. If the recipe
   calls for two sticks of butter, how many
   sticks of butter will she need for her recipe? _____

4. How many sticks of butter would she
   need if she wanted to cut the recipe in half? _____

DAY 15

Solve mentally.

1. 51 − 18 = _____
2. 96 = _____ + 37
3. 42 − 19 = _____
4. 83 = _____ + 44
5. 73 − 20 = _____
6. 71 = _____ + 52

7. Look at the chart. How can you predict the doubles of 26, 27, and 28?

_____

_____

_____

_____

Number	Double that number	Answer
5	5 + 5	10
15	15 + 15	30
6	6 + 6	12
16	16 + 16	32
7	7 + 7	14
17	17 + 17	34
8	8 + 8	16
18	18 + 18	36

DAY 16

Fill in the blanks. Use each sum to find the next.

1. 2 + 2 = _____
   _____ + 6 = _____
   _____ + 8 = _____
   _____ + 10 = _____
   _____ + 12 = _____
   _____ + _____ = 54

Complete these patterns.

2. 1, 3, 5, 7, 9, _____, 21

3. 3, 7, 11, 15, 19, _____, 39

4. 27, 24, 21, 18, _____, 0

Day 17

Write two equations using some or all the numbers.

1. 2, 3, 6, 12   _____ and _____

2. 2, 4, 8, 16   _____ and _____

3. 2, 3, 4, 7, 12, 14   _____ and _____

4. 2, 3, 5, 10, 15   _____ and _____

5. How many minutes in 1 hour? _____

6. How many minutes in $\frac{1}{4}$ hour? _____

7. How many minutes in $\frac{1}{2}$ hour? _____

8. How many minutes in 2 hours? _____

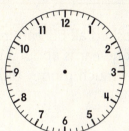

Day 18

Find the answers. Look for a pattern.

1.
```
   16        32        16
 + 16      - 16       × 2
```
32 ÷ 2 = _____

2.
```
   19        38        19
 + 19      - 19       × 2
```
38 ÷ 2 = _____

3.
```
   13        26        13
 + 13      - 13       × 2
```
26 ÷ 2 = _____

4. Look at these figures. Will the square fit inside the circle? Explain. _____

   _____

   _____

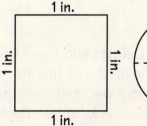

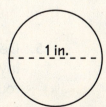

5. Will the circle fit inside the square? Explain. _____

   _____

DAY 19

Fill in the blanks.

1. _____ × 4 = 8
   + _____ × 7 = _____
   —————————————
   22

2. 8 × _____ = _____
   + 4 × _____ = _____
   —————————————
   24

3. 3 × _____ = _____
   + 2 × _____ = _____
   —————————————
   30

4. Andy deposited all his earnings for two weeks.
   Each week he earns about $120.
   About how much money did he deposit? _____

DAY 20

1. Use the numbers 2, 3, 5, 6, 7, and 8. Make as many differences as possible.

   _____

   _____

   _____

Fill in the blanks.

2. 5 × _____ = 20
   + _____ × 3 = 15
   ——————————————
   35

3. 7 × _____ = 35
   + _____ × 5 = 30
   ——————————————
   65

4. 10 × 5 = _____
   + _____ × 4 = 40
   ——————————————
   90

5. Delores and Elena wanted to have a party. They
   invited four friends to join them. Delores bought
   four packs of three juicy drinks and Elena bought
   six packs of two cookies. Was there enough for
   each person at the party to have two of each? _____

6. How many more packs of cookies should Elena
   buy so that each person at the party can have three cookies? _____

1	2	3	4	5	6	7	8	9	10
11	12	13	14	15	16	17	18	19	20
21	22	23	24	25	26	27	28	29	30
31	32	33	34	35	36	37	38	39	40
41	42	43	44	45	46	47	48	49	50
51	52	53	54	55	56	57	58	59	60
61	62	63	64	65	66	67	68	69	70
71	72	73	74	75	76	77	78	79	80
81	82	83	84	85	86	87	88	89	90
91	92	93	94	95	96	97	98	99	100

1. Write five things that come in 3's. Write a multiplication story for each.

   (Example: 2 traffic signals with 3 lights in each = 6 lights, so $2 \times 3 = 6$.)

   _____

   _____

   _____

   _____

   _____

2. Write three sentences about what you see in the pattern of multiples of three on

   the 100 chart. _____

   _____

   _____

   _____

   _____

MONTHLY ASSESSMENT

Fill in the blanks.

1. $\begin{array}{r} 17 \\ +17 \\ \hline \end{array}$ $\begin{array}{r} 34 \\ -17 \\ \hline \end{array}$ $\begin{array}{r} 17 \\ \times 2 \\ \hline \end{array}$ $34 \times 2 = \underline{\hspace{1cm}}$

2. $\begin{array}{r} 18 \\ +18 \\ \hline \end{array}$ $\begin{array}{r} 36 \\ -18 \\ \hline \end{array}$ $\begin{array}{r} 18 \\ \times 2 \\ \hline \end{array}$ $36 \times 2 = \underline{\hspace{1cm}}$

3. $\begin{array}{r} 12 \\ +12 \\ \hline \end{array}$ $\begin{array}{r} 24 \\ -12 \\ \hline \end{array}$ $\begin{array}{r} 12 \\ \times 2 \\ \hline \end{array}$ $24 \times 2 = \underline{\hspace{1cm}}$

4. $50 - 19 = \underline{\hspace{1cm}}$

5. $96 = \underline{\hspace{1cm}} + 33$

6. $41 - 19 = \underline{\hspace{1cm}}$

7. $83 = \underline{\hspace{1cm}} + 44$

8. $70 - 17 = \underline{\hspace{1cm}}$

9. $71 = \underline{\hspace{1cm}} + 51$

10. $2 \times \underline{\hspace{1cm}} = 12$

11. $3 \times 5 = \underline{\hspace{1cm}}$

12. $9 \times \underline{\hspace{1cm}} = 18$

13. $\underline{\hspace{1cm}} \times 2 = 16$

14. $3 \times \underline{\hspace{1cm}} = 12$

15. $7 \times 5 = \underline{\hspace{1cm}}$

16. $6 \times 5 = \underline{\hspace{1cm}}$

17. $9 \times 5 = \underline{\hspace{1cm}}$

18. $8 \times \underline{\hspace{1cm}} = 40$

19. $25 \div \underline{\hspace{1cm}} = 12 \text{ R}\underline{\hspace{1cm}}$

20. $\underline{\hspace{1cm}} \div 2 = 6 \text{ R}\underline{\hspace{1cm}}$

21. $27 \div 2 = \underline{\hspace{1cm}}$

22. $(12 \times 2) + 1 = \underline{\hspace{1cm}}$

23. $(\underline{\hspace{1cm}} \times 2) + \underline{\hspace{1cm}} = 13$

24. $(\underline{\hspace{1cm}} \times \underline{\hspace{1cm}}) + 1 = 27$

25. $(\underline{\hspace{1cm}} \times \underline{\hspace{1cm}}) + \underline{\hspace{1cm}} = 28$

Monthly Assessment

1. How can you make 56¢ with these coins? _____

   _____

2. What coins would you ask for if you wanted this collection to total $1.50?

   _____

3. To get from San Francisco to Sacramento, your car uses
   four gallons of gas. How much gas would it take to go from
   San Francisco to Sacramento and then back to San Francisco? _____

4. How much gas would it take your car to make
   two round trips between San Francisco and Sacramento? _____

5. Randee is thinking of a number. She calls it "x."
   Each phrase describes the number. What is the number?
   x is less than 20
   x ÷ 2 has no remainder
   x ÷ 3 has no remainder
   x ÷ 4 has no remainder
   x ÷ 5 has a remainder of 2   x = _____

Get a coin or a counter with _heads_ on one side and _tails_ on the other.

6. Predict how many times your coin would land
   heads-up if you tossed it one hundred times. _____

7. Toss your coin ten times and tally your results.
   Do you want to change your prediction? Why or why not?

   _____

MONTHLY ASSESSMENT

1. Show all the ways you could make 31¢ with these coins.

   _____

   _____

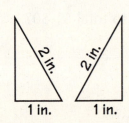

2. Look at these figures. How could you make an equilateral

   triangle with these triangles? _____

   _____

   _____

3. Show how you could fill the hexagon with
   right triangles. Explain why you could do it.

   _____

   _____

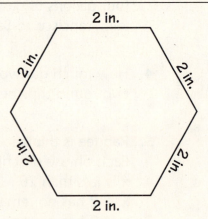

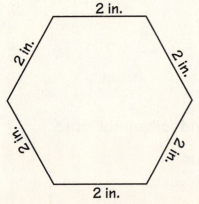

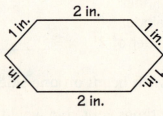

4. Draw as many lines of symmetry as you can in each hexagon.
   Why do you think the lines of symmetry are not the same?

   _____

5. How many minutes are in $\frac{3}{4}$ hour? _____

DAY 1   NOVEMBER

Use the Counting Tape to solve the problems.

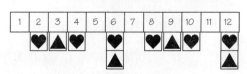

1. What multiples of 2 are shown?

   _____

2. What multiples of 3 are shown? _____

3. What multiples of both 2 and 3 are shown? _____

Complete the pattern.

4. ♡ ♡ △ ♡ ♡ △ ♡ ___ ___ ___ ___ ___ ♡

DAY 2

Use the Counting Tape to solve the problems.

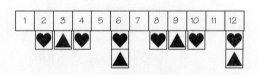

1. Write a multiplication sentence and a division sentence to show how many 2's are in 12.

   _____

2. Write a multiplication sentence and a division sentence to show how many 3's are in 12.

   _____

3. Write a multiplication sentence and a division sentence to show how many 2's are in 10.

   _____

4. Make 42 cents with the fewest coins.

5. Draw a ring around the fewest coins to make 73 cents.

DAY 3

Use the Counting Tape to solve the problems.

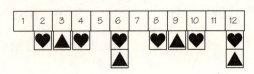

1. Think about how many 3's are in seven and how many leftovers there are. Draw a picture and write an equation for this problem.

    _____

2. Think about how many 2's are in 9 and how many leftovers there are. Draw a picture and write an equation for this problem.

    _____

3. Think about how many 3's are in 13 and how many leftovers there are. Draw a picture and write an equation for this problem.

    _____

    ☐ ☐ ☐ ☐ ☐ ☐

4. Look at these figures. How many sides are in each figure? _____

5. How many sides altogether? _____

6. How did you get your answer? _____

    _____

DAY 4

Fill in the blanks.

1. $2 \times 3 =$ _____

    $3 \times$ _____ $= 6$

2. $2 \times 6 =$ _____

    $6 \times$ _____ $= 12$

3. $2 \times 4 =$ _____

    $4 \times$ _____ $= 8$

4. $3 \times 4 =$ _____

    $4 \times$ _____ $= 12$

5. In September, our class collected $456.
    By the end of October we had $1457.
    How much money did we collect in October? _____

6. How much more will we need to collect to have $2000? _____

DAY 5

Fill in the blanks.

1. $12 \div 3 =$ _____   2. $6 \div 3 =$ _____

3. $12 \div$ _____ $= 4$ 4. $6 \div$ _____ $= 3$

5. $10 \div 2 =$ _____   6. $4 \div 2 =$ _____

7. $10 \div$ _____ $= 2$ 8. $3 \div$ _____ $= 1$

9. $8 \div$ _____ $= 2$ 10. $2 \div$ _____ $= 1$

11. $8 \div$ _____ $= 4$ 12. $4 \div$ _____ $= 1$

13. Bret says he wants to have a birthday party. Bret's mom and dad say he cannot have more than 20 people at the party. At the party he and the other children will be playing games in groups of 2 or 3. Bret wants to be sure that nobody is left out of any game. How many people should Bret have at his party, including himself? Give more than one answer.

_____

DAY 6

Fill in the blanks. Look for a pattern.

1. $5 \times 2 =$ _____   2. $5 \times 2 =$ _____   3. $6 \times 2 =$ _____

   $10 \times 2 =$ _____ $15 \times 2 =$ _____ $12 \times 2 =$ _____

   $20 \times 2 =$ _____ $25 \times 2 =$ _____ $18 \times 2 =$ _____

   $30 \times 2 =$ _____ $35 \times 2 =$ _____ $24 \times 2 =$ _____

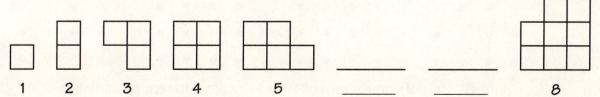

1   2   3   4   5   _____   _____   8

4. Think of a pattern that starts like this. Then use your pattern to fill in the blanks.

5. How did you figure out the pattern? _____

_____

DAY 7

Fill in the blanks. Look for a pattern.

1. $4 \times 2 =$ _____

   $8 \times 2 =$ _____

   $12 \times 2 =$ _____

   $16 \times 2 =$ _____

   $20 \times 2 =$ _____

2. $7 \times 2 =$ _____

   $14 \times 2 =$ _____

   $21 \times 2 =$ _____

   $28 \times 2 =$ _____

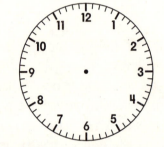

3. Set the clock to 7:53. How many more

   minutes until 8:00? _____

4. How do you know? _____

   _____

   _____

DAY 8

Fill in the blanks. Look for a pattern.

1. $4 \times 3 =$ _____

   $8 \times 3 =$ _____

   $16 \times 3 =$ _____

   $32 \times 3 =$ _____

2. $6 \times 2 =$ _____

   $12 \times 2 =$ _____

   $24 \times 2 =$ _____

   $48 \times 2 =$ _____

3. Connect four dots on each geoboard to make different quadrilaterals. Which of

   your quadrilaterals have a line of symmetry? How do you know? _____

   _____

   _____

DAY 9

Fill in the blanks. Look for a pattern.

1. 11 × 2 = _____   2. 12 × 2 = _____   3. 13 × 2 = _____

4. 14 × 2 = _____   5. 15 × 2 = _____   6. 16 × 2 = _____

7. 17 × 2 = _____   8. 18 × 2 = _____   9. 19 × 2 = _____

10. What strategy did you use to get the answers for problems 1 through 9?

_____

_____

11. The McMaths bought a basket of 19 oranges.
    They shared them equally among 6 friends.
    How many did each friend get and how many were left? _____ _____

12. What if they had to share 19 oranges
    among 5 friends? How many would be left over? _____

DAY 10   CHECKPOINT

1. Draw pictures showing how 12 can be divided evenly into groups of 2, 3, and 4.
   Tell a story for each picture and write an equation to go with it.

2. Tell an easy way to double each of these numbers: 25, 26, 27, 28, 29, 30.

_____

3. Show 53 cents with at least one of each kind of coin.

4. Show 10:53 on this clock.

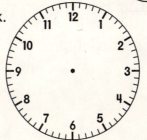

DAY 11

Fill in the blanks.

1. 10 + _____ = 100
2. 100 − 60 = _____
3. 100 − 20 = _____
4. 70 + _____ = 100
5. 30 + _____ = 100
6. 100 − 80 = _____
7. 100 − 40 = _____
8. 90 + _____ = 100
9. 50 + _____ = 100
10. 100 − 50 = _____

Continue this pattern.

11. 0, 4, 8, 12, _____, _____, _____, _____, _____

DAY 12

Fill in the blanks.

1. 35 + _____ = 100
2. _____ + 85 = 100
3. 55 + _____ = 100
4. _____ + 65 = 100
5. 75 + _____ = 100
6. _____ + 85 = 100
7. 95 + _____ = 100
8. _____ + 45 = 100

9. In November, our class was marking a foot a day on the floor.

   On the fifth, the class had marked 5 feet.

   This is the same as _____ yards and _____ feet.

1 yd			2 yd		
1 ft	2 ft	3 ft	4 ft	5 ft	6 ft

10. How many more feet are needed in problem 9 to get to 3 yards? _____

DAY 13

Subtract. Look for patterns.

1. 100 − 33 = _____   2. 100 − 53 = _____

3. 100 − 38 = _____   4. 100 − 58 = _____

5. 100 − 36 = _____   6. 100 − 56 = _____

7. 100 − 31 = _____   8. 100 − 51 = _____

9. 100 − 35 = _____   10. 100 − 45 = _____

This figure is made up of squares.

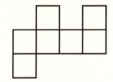

11. What is the area of the figure? _____

12. What is its perimeter? _____

DAY 14

Solve mentally.

1. 56 + _____ = 106   2. 61 + _____ = 101

3. _____ + 73 = 103   4. 82 + _____ = 122

5. 94 + _____ = 144   6. 47 + _____ = 107

7. Athena, Theo, and Samantha were picking apples at the orchard.
   Athena picked one Cortland apple for each of them.
   Theo picked three Baldwin apples for each of them.
   Samantha picked four McIntosh apples for each of them.
   How many apples did they pick altogether? _____

8. How many apples would they have if
   Theo ate his instead of sharing them? _____

DAY 15

Solve mentally.

1. $57 + \underline{\hspace{1cm}} = 123$ $123 - 57 = \underline{\hspace{1cm}}$

2. $92 + \underline{\hspace{1cm}} = 155$ $155 - 92 = \underline{\hspace{1cm}}$

3. $86 + \underline{\hspace{1cm}} = 137$ $137 - 86 = \underline{\hspace{1cm}}$

4. $63 + \underline{\hspace{1cm}} = 121$ $121 - 63 = \underline{\hspace{1cm}}$

5. Ellie is playing a game. She has to draw 4 cards, then make as many addition and subtraction problems as she can. She gets extra points if her answer is also one of her cards. She draws cards numbered 2, 4, 7, and 9. What problems can she make?

_____

_____

6. Use Ellie's 4 cards. See how many different answers you can get with multiplication or division equations.

_____

_____

DAY 16

1. Write the multiples of 10 through 10×10. _____

_____

_____

2. What do all these answers have in common? Why do you think this is so?

_____

_____

_____

Continue the pattern.

3. 1, 3, 6, 10, _____, _____, _____, _____, 45

4. What is the rule for your pattern? _____

_____

DAY 17

Match the problems on the left with the answers on the right.

1. 10×11 140

2. 10×12 150

3. 10×13 110

4. 10×14 130

5. 10×15 120

6. Was matching the answers easy or hard? Explain. _____

_____

_____

7. On each day of school this month our class
   marked a foot on the floor. On the 23rd day we
   had marked 23 feet. How many yards and feet is that? _____

8. Express your answer to problem 7 as a mixed number. _____

DAY 18

Solve mentally.

1. $230 \times 10 =$ _____   2. _____ $\times 10 = 2500$

3. $10 \times$ _____ $= 270$ 4. $10 \times 26 =$ _____

5. _____ $\times 10 = 2100$ 6. $270 \times$ _____ $= 2700$

7. $22 \times$ _____ $= 220$ 8. $28 \times$ _____ $= 280$

9. $240 \times 10 =$ _____   10. $10 \times$ _____ $= 290$

11. Compare the figures. What is alike about these figures?

_____

_____

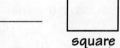
square

rectangle

12. What is different about these figures? _____

_____

_____

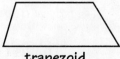
trapezoid

DAY 19

Solve mentally.

1. $2 \times 3 =$ _____ and $4 \times 3 =$ _____

2. $2 \times 6 =$ _____ and $4 \times 6 =$ _____

3. $2 \times 8 =$ _____ and $4 \times 8 =$ _____

4. $2 \times 7 =$ _____ and $4 \times 7 =$ _____

5. $2 \times 9 =$ _____ and $4 \times 9 =$ _____

6. Angela made enough cookies for her classmates to have two apiece.
   If she has twenty-seven classmates, how many cookies did she make? _____

7. What if two classmates were absent?
   How many cookies would Angela have left over? _____

DAY 20

Solve mentally.

1. $2 \times$ _____ $= 12$ 2. $2 \times 2 =$ _____

3. $2 \times 3 =$ _____   4. $20 = 4 \times$ _____

5. $23 \times 10 =$ _____   6. $17 \times 10 =$ _____

7. $4 \times 9 =$ _____   8. $30 \times 10 =$ _____

9. $3 \times 8 =$ _____   10. $27 \times 10 =$ _____

11. _____ $\times 18 = 180$ 12. $10 \times$ _____ $= 130$

13. Julie is a waitress at a restaurant that sets different tables for dinner
    and for dessert. At the dinner tables, each setting has a knife, two
    forks and a spoon. At the dessert tables, a setting has two spoons.
    Julie is setting tables that require 42 pieces of silverware, 21 of which
    are spoons. How many dinner tables and dessert tables is she setting?

    _____

14. How many pieces of silverware does Julie need to set 8 dinner tables? _____

15. How many pieces of silverware does Julie
    need to set 8 dinner tables and 8 dessert tables? _____

Look for place–value patterns.

1. Fill in the table.

Tens	Ones	Number
0	0	0
0	4	4
0	8	
1	2	

1. What do you notice about the numbers? _____

2. Predict the next ten multiples of 4 using the pattern. What are the numbers?

_____

3. Shade in the multiples of 4 on the hundred chart.

4. Write about three patterns you see when looking at the multiples of 4 in your chart.

_____

_____

_____

_____

_____

_____

1	2	3	4	5	6	7	8	9	10
11	12	13	14	15	16	17	18	19	20
21	22	23	24	25	26	27	28	29	30
31	32	33	34	35	36	37	38	39	40
41	42	43	44	45	46	47	48	49	50
51	52	53	54	55	56	57	58	59	60
61	62	63	64	65	66	67	68	69	70
71	72	73	74	75	76	77	78	79	80
81	82	83	84	85	86	87	88	89	90
91	92	93	94	95	96	97	98	99	100

MONTHLY ASSESSMENT

Use the hundred chart to help you solve the problems.

1. Put an X on each multiple of 4 on the hundred chart.

2. What do you notice about the multiples of 2 and 4? _____

    _____

    _____

3. What numbers in the chart are multiples of 2, 3, and 4? _____

    _____

1	2	3	4	5	6	7	8	9	10
11	12	13	14	15	16	17	18	19	20
21	22	23	24	25	26	27	28	29	30
31	32	33	34	35	36	37	38	39	40
41	42	43	44	45	46	47	48	49	50
51	52	53	54	55	56	57	58	59	60
61	62	63	64	65	66	67	68	69	70
71	72	73	74	75	76	77	78	79	80
81	82	83	84	85	86	87	88	89	90
91	92	93	94	95	96	97	98	99	100

Solve mentally.

4. $12 \div \underline{\hspace{1cm}} = 4$

5. $3 \div \underline{\hspace{1cm}} = 1$

6. $8 \div \underline{\hspace{1cm}} = 2$

7. $10 + \underline{\hspace{1cm}} = 100$

8. $100 - \underline{\hspace{1cm}} = 80$

9. $\underline{\hspace{1cm}} + 30 = 100$

10. $\underline{\hspace{1cm}} + 5 = 100$

11. $15 + \underline{\hspace{1cm}} = 100$

12. $65 + 35 = \underline{\hspace{1cm}}$

13. $94 + \underline{\hspace{1cm}} = 144$

14. $87 + \underline{\hspace{1cm}} = 117$

15. $\underline{\hspace{1cm}} + 90 = 115$

16. $5 \times \underline{\hspace{1cm}} = 10$

    $10 \times 2 = \underline{\hspace{1cm}}$

    $\underline{\hspace{1cm}} \times 2 = 40$

17. $6 \times 3 = \underline{\hspace{1cm}}$

    $\underline{\hspace{1cm}} \times 3 = 36$

    $24 \times 3 = \underline{\hspace{1cm}}$

18. $1 \times \underline{\hspace{1cm}} = 4$

    $\underline{\hspace{1cm}} \times 4 = 8$

    $4 \times 4 = \underline{\hspace{1cm}}$

19. $100 - 33 = \underline{\hspace{1cm}}$

    $100 - \underline{\hspace{1cm}} = 47$

20. $100 - 27 = \underline{\hspace{1cm}}$

    $100 - \underline{\hspace{1cm}} = 53$

21. $100 - 48 = \underline{\hspace{1cm}}$

    $100 - \underline{\hspace{1cm}} = 32$

22. $57 + \underline{\hspace{1cm}} = 123$

    $123 - 57 = \underline{\hspace{1cm}}$

23. $98 + \underline{\hspace{1cm}} = 122$

    $122 - 98 = \underline{\hspace{1cm}}$

24. $75 + \underline{\hspace{1cm}} = 109$

    $109 - 75 = \underline{\hspace{1cm}}$

25. $10 \times 230 = \underline{\hspace{1cm}}$

26. $10 \times \underline{\hspace{1cm}} = 1600$

27. $\underline{\hspace{1cm}} \times 120 = 1200$

MONTHLY ASSESSMENT

In problems 1–4 each table seats 3 people.
Use this fact to solve the problems.

Breakfast

Lunch

Dinner

1. Joe's Cafe serves only breakfast and has 10 tables.
   How many pieces of tableware do they need at Joe's Cafe? _____

2. Annie's Place serves only lunch and has 20 tables.
   How many pieces of tableware do they need at Annie's Place? _____

3. The Ritzy Restaurant serves lunch and dinner and has 20 tables.
   How many pieces of tableware do they need at the Ritzy Restaurant?
   They do not use the same tableware for lunch and dinner.

   _____

4. At the class picnic, they want to organize teams
   for a 3-legged race and a 4-person relay. Can
   everyone participate in both if 24 people are at the picnic? _____

5. How many 3-legged race teams will there be? _____

6. How many 4-person relay teams will there be? _____

7. What if there were 26 people at the picnic? Could everyone participate
   in both events? If not, which one could they all participate in?

   _____

8. What if there were 28 people at the picnic? Could everyone participate

   in both events? If not, which one could they all participate in? _____

9. Show all the ways the class of 24 could line up in equal rows
   for the class picture.

MONTHLY ASSESSMENT

The figures in this pattern are made of squares.
Use that fact to help you solve the problems.

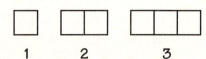

1   2   3

1. What is the perimeter of the first figure? _____

2. How many more units are in the perimeter of the second figure? _____

3. Why isn't the perimeter of the second figure twice as long as the perimeter of the first? _____

   _____

   _____

4. Does the area of the figures change in the same way the perimeter does? Explain.

   _____

   _____

   _____

5. How much money is shown here? _____

6. What one coin could you add to have a total of $1.45? _____

7. How much money would be left if you removed one of each kind of coin? _____

Use this clock to help you solve the problems.

8. What time is it? _____

9. How long will it be until the

   next hour? _____

10. What time will it be in 5 minutes? _____

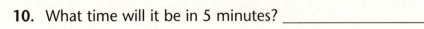

11. How many feet are in 2 yards? _____

12. How many yards are in 8 feet? _____

DAY 1

Use the Counting Tape to solve these problems.

1. What multiples of 4 are shown here? _____

2. What multiples of 5 are shown here? _____

3. What multiples of both 4 and 5 are shown here? _____

4. The first thirteen circles follow a pattern. Think of a rule for this pattern, then work with the last seven circles so that all circles match your rule.

DAY 2

Write a division number sentence and show the solution for each problem.

1. How many 4's are in 28? _____

2. How many 4's are in 36? _____

3. How many 4's are in 24? _____

4. How many 3's are in 18? _____

5. How many 3's are in 21? _____

6. How many 3's are in 24? _____

7. If Tony has to mark off 18 feet for his booth at the fair, how many times will he put the yardstick down? _____

8. What if Tony's booth was 20 feet long? _____

DAY 3

Fill in the blanks.

1. $3 \times 4 = \underline{\hspace{1.5cm}}$

   $4 \times \underline{\hspace{1.5cm}} = 12$

   $12 \div 3 = \underline{\hspace{1.5cm}}$

   $12 \div \underline{\hspace{1.5cm}} = 3$

2. $5 \times 4 = \underline{\hspace{1.5cm}}$

   $4 \times \underline{\hspace{1.5cm}} = 20$

   $20 \div 4 = \underline{\hspace{1.5cm}}$

   $20 \div 5 = \underline{\hspace{1.5cm}}$

3. $7 \times 4 = \underline{\hspace{1.5cm}}$

   $4 \times \underline{\hspace{1.5cm}} = 28$

   $28 \div \underline{\hspace{1.5cm}} = 7$

   $\underline{\hspace{1.5cm}} \div 7 = 4$

4. $4 \times \underline{\hspace{1.5cm}} = 32$

   $8 \times \underline{\hspace{1.5cm}} = 32$

   $\underline{\hspace{1.5cm}} \div 8 = 4$

   $32 \div \underline{\hspace{1.5cm}} = 8$

6. Use the geoboards. Connect dots to make 3 different pentagons.

DAY 4

1. $5 \times \underline{\hspace{1.5cm}} = 50$

   $10 \times \underline{\hspace{1.5cm}} = 50$

   $50 \div 5 = \underline{\hspace{1.5cm}}$

   $\underline{\hspace{1.5cm}} \div 10 = 5$

2. $4 \times \underline{\hspace{1.5cm}} = 24$

   $6 \times \underline{\hspace{1.5cm}} = 24$

   $\underline{\hspace{1.5cm}} \div 4 = 6$

   $24 \div 6 = \underline{\hspace{1.5cm}}$

3. $5 \times \underline{\hspace{1.5cm}} = 35$

   $\underline{\hspace{1.5cm}} \times 5 = 35$

   $35 \div \underline{\hspace{1.5cm}} = 5$

   $35 \div 5 = \underline{\hspace{1.5cm}}$

4. $4 \times \underline{\hspace{1.5cm}} = 36$

   $9 \times 4 = \underline{\hspace{1.5cm}}$

   $36 \div 9 = \underline{\hspace{1.5cm}}$

   $36 \div \underline{\hspace{1.5cm}} = 9$

5. Aldwin has 51 marbles. He plays a game where 4 people start with an equal numbers of marbles. How many will each player get? $\underline{\hspace{1.5cm}}$

6. How many marbles will not be used in the game? $\underline{\hspace{1.5cm}}$

DAY 5

Use the Counting Tape.

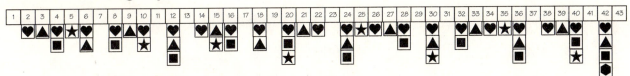

1. How many whole groups of 4 are in 38? _____

2. How many whole groups of 3 are in 25? _____

3. How many whole groups of 5 are in 43? _____

4. Luis is playing a game with his friends. Each player draws five digit-cards. He or she uses any four of the cards to make a four-digit number. The person with the lowest four-digit number wins. Luis has drawn 0, 6, 9, and 5. He has one more draw. His opponent has 1, 2, 0, and 9. What card will help Luis the most? Explain how you made your decision.

_____

_____

DAY 6

Use the Counting Tape.

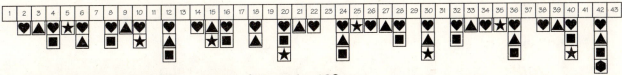

1. How many whole groups of 4 are in 42? _____

2. How many whole groups of 3 are in 42? _____

3. How many whole groups of 5 are in 24? _____

You have $2760 in the fewest possible play–money bills. Use this fact to help you solve the problems.

4. How many $1000 bills are there? _____

5. How many $100 bills are there? _____

6. How many $10 bills are there? _____

7. How many $1 bills are there? _____

8. If this was real money, you couldn't have $1000 bills because they are no longer in circulation. How many $100 bills would you have? _____

DAY 7

Fill in the blanks. Look for a pattern.

1. 1000 − 100 = _____
2. 700 + 300 = _____
3. 1000 − 200 = _____
4. 600 + 400 = _____
5. 1000 − 300 = _____
6. 800 + 200 = _____
7. 1000 − 400 = _____
8. 900 + 100 = _____
9. 1000 − 500 = _____
10. 500 + 500 = _____

11. Ms. Kay is timing a test. It has been 67 minutes since the test started. How many hours has it been and how many minutes are left over? _____

12. How much longer will it be until the 2-hour test is over? _____

DAY 8

Fill in the blanks. Look for a pattern.

1. 450 + _____ = 1000
2. 350 + _____ = 1000
3. 250 + _____ = 1000
4. 150 + _____ = 1000
5. 50 + _____ = 1000
6. 550 + _____ = 1000
7. 650 + _____ = 1000
8. 750 + _____ = 1000
9. 850 + _____ = 1000
10. 950 + _____ = 1000

11. Some geometric figures can be split exactly in half with a line of symmetry. Use this fact to help you solve the problem. Which of these has a least one line of symmetry?

_____

DAY 9

Fill in the blanks. Look for a pattern.

1. 1000 − 350 = _____   2. 1000 − 250 = _____

3. 1000 − 150 = _____   4. 1000 − 50 = _____

5. 1000 − 550 = _____   6. 1000 − 650 = _____

7. 1000 − 750 = _____   8. 1000 − 850 = _____

9. Liz went to work with one dollar, two quarters, one dime, and two pennies. She came home with five twenty-dollar bills, three quarters, ten nickels and seven pennies. How much more money did Liz have when she came home? _____

DAY 10   CHECKPOINT

Solve mentally.

1. 1100 − 450 = _____   2. 750 + _____ = 1000

3. 1550 − 600 = _____   4. _____ + 600 = 1000

5. 850 + 850 = _____   6. 1000 − _____ = 650

7. 1200 − 750 = _____   8. _____ − 150 = 850

9. How many whole groups of 4 are in 25? _____

10. How many whole groups of 6 are in 25? _____

11. How many whole groups of 5 are in 25? _____

12. What number can you use to double your money, cut your worries in half, and split your dessert evenly with a friend? _____

13. Write a convincing argument that your answer is correct. _____

_____

_____

_____

DAY 11

Solve mentally.

1. 20 × 1 = _____
2. 20 × 2 = _____
3. 20 × 3 = _____
4. 20 × 4 = _____
5. 20 × 5 = _____
6. 20 × 6 = _____
7. 20 × 7 = _____
8. 20 × 8 = _____
9. 20 × 9 = _____
10. 20 × 10 = _____

Complete these patterns

11. 0, 3, 6, 9, 12, _____, 33.
12. 30, 28, 26, 24, _____, 0.

DAY 12

Solve mentally.

1. 11 × 2 = _____ and 22 × 10 = _____
2. 12 × 2 = _____ and 24 × 10 = _____
3. 13 × 2 = _____ and 26 × 10 = _____
4. 14 × 2 = _____ and 28 × 10 = _____
5. 15 × 2 = _____ and 30 × 10 = _____
6. 16 × 2 = _____ and 32 × 10 = _____
7. 17 × 2 = _____ and 34 × 10 = _____
8. 18 × 2 = _____ and 36 × 10 = _____
9. 19 × 2 = _____ and 38 × 10 = _____
10. 20 × 2 = _____ and 40 × 10 = _____

11. If a dollar is 100 cents, what fraction shows $0.37? _____

12. What fraction of a dollar is $0.25? Write this fraction two ways. _____ or _____

13. Write $\frac{35}{100}$ in money notation. _____

14. Write $\frac{1}{2}$ in money notation. _____

DAY 13

Solve mentally.

1. 20 × 10 = _____ so 20 × 20 = _____

2. 21 × 10 = _____ so 21 × 20 = _____

3. 22 × 10 = _____ so 22 × 20 = _____

4. 23 × 10 = _____ so 23 × 20 = _____

5. 24 × 10 = _____ so 24 × 20 = _____

6. 25 × 10 = _____ so 25 × 20 = _____

7. 26 × 10 = _____ so 26 × 20 = _____

8. 27 × 10 = _____ so 27 × 20 = _____

9. Look at these figures.
   Which one is the quadrilateral? _____

10. Which one is the triangle? _____

11. Which one is the pentagon? _____

12. Which one is the hexagon? _____

13. What clues did you use to identify the shapes? _____

_____

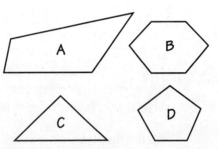

DAY 14

Solve mentally. Use the first problem in each pair to help you solve the second one.

1. 240 = 20 × _____   240 ÷ 20 = _____

2. 180 = 10 × _____   180 ÷ 10 = _____

3. 340 = 20 × _____   340 ÷ 20 = _____

4. 150 = 10 × _____   140 ÷ 10 = _____

5. 200 = 10 × _____   180 ÷ 20 = _____

6. Roseanna needs fourteen feet of fabric to make a club flag.
   How many yards of the fabric should her mom buy?   _____

DAY 15

Fill in the blanks. Use the first problem in each pair to help you solve the second one.

1. $10 \times \underline{\hspace{1cm}} = 20$ $20 \times 2 = \underline{\hspace{1cm}}$

2. $10 \times \underline{\hspace{1cm}} = 40$ $20 \times 4 = \underline{\hspace{1cm}}$

3. $10 \times \underline{\hspace{1cm}} = 50$ $20 \times 5 = \underline{\hspace{1cm}}$

4. $10 \times \underline{\hspace{1cm}} = 80$ $20 \times 8 = \underline{\hspace{1cm}}$

5. $10 \times \underline{\hspace{1cm}} = 60$ $60 \div \underline{\hspace{1cm}} = 10$

6. $20 \times \underline{\hspace{1cm}} = 160$ $160 \div 20 = \underline{\hspace{1cm}}$

7. $20 \times \underline{\hspace{1cm}} = 100$ $100 \div 20 = \underline{\hspace{1cm}}$

8. $10 \times \underline{\hspace{1cm}} = 90$ $90 \div \underline{\hspace{1cm}} = 10$

6	2	**15**	12	3	**20**	4	5

9. Use only the numbers in the box to write four equations using multiplication or division. _____

_____

_____

10. Use only the numbers in the box to write four equations using addition or subtraction. _____

_____

_____

11. If the Daily Depositor collects $20 times each day's date, how much will be collected from December 18 through December 31? _____

12. How much money will the Daily Depositor collect from December 1 through December 17? _____

13. Why would the Daily Depositor collect so much more at the end of the month than at the beginning?

_____

_____

MONTHLY ASSESSMENT

1. Study the calendar. Name the shapes used to make the calendar pattern.

    _____

2. Use A's and B's to describe the shading pattern in the calendar. _____

    _____

3. Use A's and B's to describe the pattern of the circles. _____

    _____

4. Predict the last piece if the month had 45 days. _____

    _____

5. What special patterns do you see on multiples? _____

    _____

    _____

    _____

MONTHLY ASSESSMENT

Use the Counting Tape.

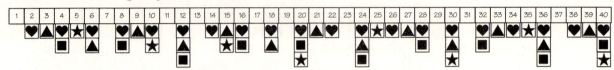

1. What marker is on the multiples of 3? _____

2. What marker is on the multiples of 4? _____

3. What marker is on the multiples of 5? _____

4. What common multiples of 3 and 4 are on this tape? _____

5. What common multiples of 3 and 5 are on this tape? _____

6. What common multiples of 4 and 5 are on this tape? _____

7. Are there any common multiples of 3, 4, and 5 on this tape? If not, name one. _____

Fill in the blanks.

8. $7 \times$ _____ $= 56$ $56 \div 7 =$ _____

9. $9 \times$ _____ $= 54$ $54 \div 9 =$ _____

10. _____ $\times 4 = 12$ _____ $\times 4 = 24$

11. _____ $\times 10 = 40$ _____ $\times 10 = 80$

12. $10 \times 10 =$ _____ $20 \times 10 =$ _____

13. $10 \times$ _____ $= 300$ $20 \times$ _____ $= 600$

14. $11 \times 2 =$ _____   _____ $\times 10 = 220$

15. $12 \times 3 =$ _____   _____ $\times 10 = 360$

16. $950 +$ _____ $= 1000$ $1000 -$ _____ $= 950$

17. $150 + 850 =$ _____   _____ $- 150 = 850$

18. $600 +$ _____ $= 1000$ $1000 - 600 =$ _____

19. $10 \times$ _____ $= 200$ $200 \div 10 =$ _____

20. $12 \times$ _____ $= 240$ $240 \div 12 =$ _____

21. _____ $\times 20 = 300$ $300 \div$ _____ $= 20$

MONTHLY ASSESSMENT

You are a florist and you have these flowers to use.

1. How many bouquets with 6 flowers can you make? _____

2. You can make twelve 2-flower bouquets. Think about all the other bouquet sizes you can make. Tell what bouquets you can make using all the flowers.

    _____

    _____

3. How many more flowers do you need
    in order to make five 5-flower bouquets? _____

Use each digit–card only once in each problem.

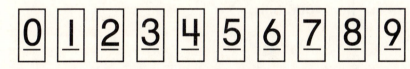

4. What is the smallest 4-digit number you can make? _____

5. What is the largest 4-digit number you can make? _____

6. Which cards would you use to show two pairs of factors with the same product?

    _____

7. Make two numbers with a sum of 10,000. _____

8. There will be 240 seats on the lawn for graduation. Show all the ways you can

    make equal rows of chairs if there are at least 5 rows. _____

    _____

    _____

9. What is the greatest number of rows you can make? _____

MONTHLY ASSESSMENT

Use the diagram.

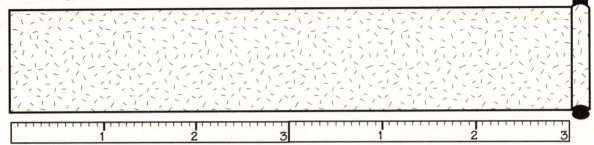

1. How many more yardsticks are needed to measure 4 $\frac{1}{2}$ yards? _____

2. Jody wants to buy 1 $\frac{1}{3}$ yards of fabric. Mark where the clerk should cut.

3. How many yards should you buy if you need 5 feet to make a banner?

   _____

4. How many feet are in 3 $\frac{1}{3}$ yards? _____

You have $1106 in play-money bills. Use this fact to help you solve the problems. (There are no $1000 bills.)

5. What would be the fewest bills for this amount? _____

6. How much more money is needed to have $2000? _____

7. If you want to add the fewest possible bills to get to $2000, which would you add?

   _____

Use this clock.

8. What time is it? _____

9. The test started at 8:30. How long has it been

   going on? _____

10. The test ends at 10:15. How much longer until

    it's over? _____

11. How long is this test in hours and minutes? _____

Multiply.

1. $2 \times 5 =$ _____   2. $3 \times 5 =$ _____   3. $5 \times 5 =$ _____

4. $7 \times 5 =$ _____   5. $4 \times 5 =$ _____   6. $6 \times 5 =$ _____

7. $10 \times 5 =$ _____   8. $8 \times 5 =$ _____   9. $9 \times 5 =$ _____

Continue the pattern.

10. 1, 5, 11, 23, _____, _____, _____, 383

DAY 2 •

Fill in the blanks.

1. $7 \times 3 =$ _____   2. $12 \div 4 =$ _____

3. $36 \div 4 =$ _____   4. $32 \div 4 =$ _____

5. $27 \div 3 =$ _____   6. $28 \div 4 =$ _____

7. $18 \div 3 =$ _____   8. $36 \div 9 =$ _____

9. $3 \times 9 =$ _____   10. $9 \times 4 =$ _____

11. $10 \times 4 =$ _____   12. $3 \times 4 =$ _____

Fill in the blank spaces in this coin chart for 61¢.

	Quarters	Dimes	Nickels	Pennies	Coins
13.	2	1		1	4
14.	1	2		1	7
15.	1		5	1	8
16.		0			9
17.		0			5
18.		1	3		16

DAY 3

Divide.

1. $8 \div 4 = $ _____   2. $9 \div 3 = $ _____

3. $10 \div 2 = $ _____   4. $12 \div 3 = $ _____

5. $12 \div 6 = $ _____   6. $15 \div 5 = $ _____

7. $14 \div 2 = $ _____   8. $18 \div 3 = $ _____

9. $16 \div 8 = $ _____   10. $21 \div 7 = $ _____

11. $18 \div 2 = $ _____   12. $24 \div 3 = $ _____

13. Look at the two figures. Tell two ways that the figures are alike. _____

_____

14. Tell two ways that the figures are different. _____

_____

DAY 4

Multiply. Look for a pattern.

1. $2 \times 4 = $ _____ $4 \times 4 = $ _____

2. $3 \times 4 = $ _____ $6 \times 4 = $ _____

3. $4 \times 4 = $ _____ $8 \times 4 = $ _____

4. $5 \times 4 = $ _____ $10 \times 4 = $ _____

5. $6 \times 4 = $ _____ $12 \times 4 = $ _____

6. In September, Garrod noticed that the Daily Depositor had collected $465 in play money. In October the bank collected $992. In November the bank collected $4650. If the bank had $16,027 dollars on January 1, how much did it collect in December? _____

7. If the play-money set had no thousand-dollar bills, how many hundreds would the class need to show that amount? _____

DAY 5

Divide.

1. 10 ÷ 5 = _____
2. 15 ÷ 5 = _____
3. 20 ÷ 5 = _____
4. 25 ÷ 5 = _____
5. 30 ÷ 5 = _____
6. 35 ÷ 5 = _____
7. 40 ÷ 5 = _____
8. 45 ÷ 5 = _____
9. 50 ÷ 5 = _____
10. 55 ÷ 5 = _____

11. Describe a pattern in the quotients for problems 1 through 10. _____

    _____

    _____

12. There are twelve pencils in a box. If Mrs. Busa
    needs eighteen pencils, how many boxes must she buy? _____

13. A truck will hold 8.1 cubic yards of top soil. The
    garden center only delivers full loads. If Ms. Doveen needs
    15 cubic yards of soil, how many truckloads must she order? _____

14. Write two sentences comparing problems 12 and 13. _____

    _____

    _____

DAY 6

3		4		3		36		6	
	9		6	12		4	8	**48**	27

1. Pick two factors and a product from this box. Use each number only
   once to write a multiplication equation. Do this four times to write
   four different multiplication problems.

   _____

Continue the pattern.

2. 20, 24, 28, 32, _____, _____, _____, _____, 52

DAY 7

Use any 6 of the numbers listed. Write two multiplication and two division equations.

1. 4, 5, 7, 8, 28, 32, 40 _____

_____

2. 4, 5, 8, 9, 32, 36, 45 _____

_____

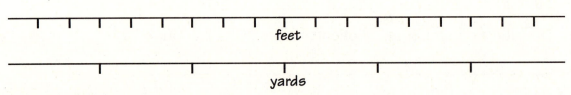

feet

yards

Use the diagram to help you fill in the blanks.

3. $3\frac{1}{3}$ yards = _____ feet

4. $4\frac{2}{3}$ yards = _____ feet

5. 18 feet = _____ yards

6. 4 feet = _____ yards

DAY 8

Write 3, 4, or 5 in each blank to make the equations true.

1. 12 ÷ _____ = 4

2. 9 ÷ _____ = 3

3. 15 ÷ _____ = 5

4. 16 ÷ _____ = 4

5. 12 ÷ _____ = 3

6. 20 ÷ _____ = 5

7. 20 ÷ _____ = 4

8. 15 ÷ _____ = 3

9. 25 ÷ _____ = 5

10. Compare the two figures. How are the figures alike?

_____

_____

_____

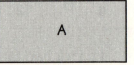

11. How are these figures different? _____

_____

_____

_____

DAY 9

Write 7, 8, or 9 in each blank to make the equations true.

1. 35 ÷ _____ = 5   **2.** 32 ÷ _____ = 4   **3.** 27 ÷ _____ = 3

4. 24 ÷ 3 = _____   **5.** 24 ÷ _____ = 3   **6.** 36 ÷ 4 = _____

7. 21 ÷ _____ = 3   **8.** 40 ÷ 5 = _____   **9.** 45 ÷ _____ = 5

10. Cecille is buying lemonade for the class party. There are 26 students in the class and each gets one cup. There are four cups in one quart. How many quart containers will she need? _____

11. If six of her classmates want orangeade instead of lemonade, how many quart containers of lemonade does Cecille need to buy now? _____

DAY 10   CHECKPOINT

21	3	9	36	7	16	27	18	10
80	4	12	6	8	48	5	49	120	28
100	24	30	20	64	40	35	25	15

1. Write at least eight division equations using the numbers in the box. You may use a number twice. _____

_____

2. There are four cups in one quart. How many cups are in 3 quarts? _____ cups

3. How many quart bottles will ten cups fill? _____

4. How many cups will be left over? _____

Write your answers as whole or mixed numbers.

5. 10 yd = _____ ft   **6.** 35 ft = _____ yd   **7.** $5\frac{1}{3}$ yd = _____ ft

8. Compare the figures. How are the figures alike? _____

_____

Rectangle

9. How are the figures different? _____

_____

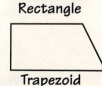
Trapezoid

DAY 11

Solve the equations.

1. $1 \times 6 = $ _____

2. $2 \times 6 = $ _____

3. $3 \times 6 = $ _____

4. $4 \times 6 = $ _____

5. $5 \times 6 = $ _____

6. Use the equations in problems 1 through 5 to label each picture.

 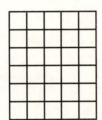 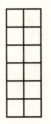 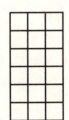 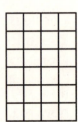

_____ _____ _____ _____ _____

Complete the pattern.

7.

DAY 12

Fill in the blanks.

1. If $3 \times 2 = $ _____, then $6 \times 2 = $ _____

2. If $3 \times 3 = $ _____, then $6 \times 3 = $ _____

3. If $3 \times 4 = $ _____, then $6 \times 4 = $ _____

4. If $3 \times 5 = $ _____, then $6 \times 5 = $ _____

5. There are four cups in one quart.
   What fractional part of a quart is 2 cups? _____

6. What fractional part of a quart is 3 cups? _____

7. What fractional part of a quart is 4 cups? _____

8. What fractional part of a quart is 5 cups? _____

DAY 13

Fill in the blanks.

1. If $3 \times 6 =$ _____, then $6 \times 6 =$ _____

2. If $3 \times 7 =$ _____, then $6 \times 7 =$ _____

3. If $3 \times 8 =$ _____, then $6 \times 8 =$ _____

4. If $3 \times 9 =$ _____, then $6 \times 9 =$ _____

5. If $3 \times 10 =$ _____, then $6 \times 10 =$ _____

6. Compare the two isosceles triangles. How are the triangles alike?

   _____

   _____

7. How are the triangles different? _____

   _____

   _____

DAY 14

Use the Counting Tape.

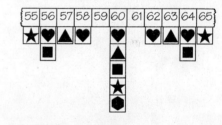

1. What numbers on the tape have 2 as

   a factor? _____

2. What numbers on the tape have 3 as a factor? _____

3. What numbers on the tape have 4 as a factor? _____

4. What numbers on the tape have 5 as a factor? _____

5. What numbers on the tape have 6 as a factor? _____

6. Orlando is the coach in charge of field day. In the morning he will put the children in groups of 7. In the afternoon he will put them in groups of 20. If he has 140 students, how many groups can he make?

   _____

7. Could Orlando have the same-size groups if he had only 70 students? Explain.

   _____

DAY 15

Use the Counting Tape.

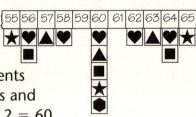

1. There are five symbols on the number 60. Each represents a factor of 60. Name the factor each symbol represents and write an equation for it. For example, heart = 2, 30 × 2 = 60.

_____

_____

There are no numerals in these statements, but there are numbers.
Find them and tell what they are.

2. Marie is the baker at the Sweet Shop. She needs to make one half-dozen bagels

   before noon. _____

3. Each batch of bagels takes one half-hour to bake and one quarter-hour to cool.

   _____

DAY 16

Fill in the blanks.

1. 2 × 30 = _____

   _____ × 29 = 58

2. 2 × _____ = 120

   _____ × 59 = 118

3. 2 × 25 = _____

   _____ × 26 = 52

4. 2 × _____ = 80

   2 × 39 = _____

5. 10 × 17 = _____

6. 24 × 20 = _____

7. 20 × 18 = _____

8. 10 × 23 = _____

9. 20 × 19 = _____

10. 20 × 27 = _____

11. 10 × 28 = _____

12. 20 × 18 = _____

13. 10 × 9 = _____

14. 20 × 29 = _____

Continue the pattern.

15. 0, 6, 12, _____, 24, _____, _____, 42, _____, 54, _____

DAY 17

Divide.

1. $110 \div 10 =$ _____
2. $120 \div 10 =$ _____
3. $130 \div 10 =$ _____
4. $220 \div 10 =$ _____
5. $240 \div 10 =$ _____
6. $260 \div 10 =$ _____
7. $140 \div 10 =$ _____
8. $150 \div 10 =$ _____
9. $280 \div 10 =$ _____

10. What do you notice about your answers? _____

_____

11. How can understanding place value help you when you divide by 10? _____

_____

_____

Fill in the blanks. Express your answers as mixed numbers.

12. 67 minutes = _____ hours

13. 13 feet = _____ yards

14. 125 cents = _____ or _____ or _____ dollars

15. 27 cups = _____ quarts

DAY 18

Fill in the blanks.

1. $10 \times 17 =$ _____
2. $24 \times 20 =$ _____
3. $160 \div 10 =$ _____
4. $220 \div 20 =$ _____
5. $240 \div 20 =$ _____
6. $300 \div 10 =$ _____
7. $10 \times 28 =$ _____
8. $20 \times 18 =$ _____

9. Compare the two figures. How are the figures alike?

_____

_____

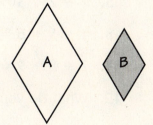

10. How are the figures different? _____

_____

Day 19

Fill in the blanks with 10 or 20 to make the equations true.

1. _____ × 30 = 300

2. _____ × 29 = 580

3. _____ × 28 = 280

4. _____ × 27 = 540

5. _____ × 13 = 260

6. _____ × 25 = 250

7. The map says it takes 83 minutes to drive from Chicago to Normal. If Justin has an hour and a half to get to Normal from Chicago, can he make it? _____

8. Will Justin have much time to spare? Explain. _____

_____

Day 20

If 10 × 8 = 80 and 20 × 8 = 160, then 30 × 8 = 240.
Find the products.

1. 10 × 3 = _____ and 20 × 3 = _____, so 30 × 3 = _____

2. 10 × 7 = _____ and 20 × 7 = _____, so 30 × 7 = _____

3. 10 × 12 = _____ and 20 × 12 = _____, so 30 × 12 = _____

4. 10 × 20 = _____ and 20 × 20 = _____, so 30 × 20 = _____

Find the sums.

5. 1 + 2 + 3 = _____   6. 2 + 3 + 4 = _____   7. 3 + 4 + 5 = _____

8. 4 + 5 + 6 = _____   9. 5 + 6 + 7 = _____   10. 6 + 7 + 8 = _____

11. 7 + 8 + 9 = _____

12. What do you notice about all the answers? _____

_____

13. Predict the next ten sums in the pattern formed in problems 5 through 11.

_____

MONTHLY ASSESSMENT

1. Name the shapes used to make the calendar pattern. _____

   _____

   _____

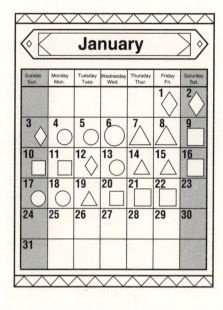

2. Use four colors. Color the calendar pieces so the pattern is a one-difference pattern.

3. January has 31 days. What piece will appear on the 31st? _____

   _____

4. Could your January 31 piece be different from your friend's January 31 piece? Explain.

   _____

   _____

   _____

5. Use stars to mark all the multiples of 6. How many multiples of 6 are on the calendar? _____

6. Use equilateral triangles and squares. Make an AAB pattern on this calendar.

7. Mark all the multiples of 5 and all the multiples of 6. On what day will both markers appear?

   _____

8. Suppose there were 37 days in January. How would your answer to problem 7 change?

   _____

MONTHLY ASSESSMENT

Fill in the blanks.

1. $6 \times$ _____ $= 30$

2. $28 \div 4 =$ _____

3. $4 \times$ _____ $= 40$

4. $50 \div$ _____ $= 10$

5. $11 \times 5 =$ _____

6. $15 \div$ _____ $= 3$

7. $4 \times$ _____ $= 24$

   $6 \times 8 =$ _____

8. $8 \times 6 =$ _____

   $16 \times$ _____ $= 96$

9. _____ $\times 6 = 42$

   $14 \times 6 =$ _____

10. $4 \times 5 =$ _____

    $8 \times$ _____ $= 40$

11. $5 \times 5 =$ _____

    $10 \times$ _____ $= 50$

12. _____ $\times 5 = 30$

    $12 \times 5 =$ _____

13. $10 \times 17 =$ _____

    $20 \times 17 =$ _____

    $20 \times 16 =$ _____

14. $10 \times 25 =$ _____

    $20 \times$ _____ $= 500$

    $20 \times 24 =$ _____

15. $10 \times 21 =$ _____

    _____ $\times 21 = 420$

    $20 \times$ _____ $= 400$

16. $180 \div 10 =$ _____

17. $240 \div$ _____ $= 24$

18. _____ $\div 10 = 68$

19. $270 \div 10 =$ _____

20. _____ $\div 10 = 14$

21. $900 \div$ _____ $= 90$

22. $20 \div 2 =$ _____

    $24 \div 2 =$ _____

    $28 \div 2 =$ _____

23. $22 \div 2 =$ _____

    $26 \div 2 =$ _____

    $30 \div 2 =$ _____

What pattern do you see in the quotients in problems 22 and 23? _____

_____

_____

List the factors of these numbers.

24. 36   1, _____, _____, _____, _____, _____, _____, _____, 36

25. 35   1, _____, _____, 35

MONTHLY ASSESSMENT

You are playing a board game. The play money is in bills of $100, $20, $10, $5, and $1.

1. You just rolled doubles, so you get $1000.
   How can you get that with the fewest bills? _____

2. You rolled 6 and 3. You landed on *Pay your neighbor 10 times your roll*. What do you pay? _____

3. How can you pay that with the fewest bills? _____

4. What if you are out of tens?
   How can you pay with the fewest bills? _____

Use the diagram to help you solve the problems.

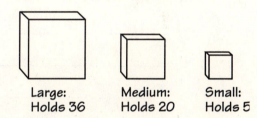

Large: Holds 36   Medium: Holds 20   Small: Holds 5

5. You are packing cookies into boxes. If you have 360 cookies, how many large boxes can you fill? _____

6. How many small boxes can you fill? _____

7. If you had 108 cookies and wanted to pack them all into same-size boxes, which box should you use? Why? _____

   _____

Abe weighs 100 pounds. Cy weighs 100 pounds. Dee weighs 100 pounds. Edie weighs 80 pounds. Foy weighs 50 pounds. Gigi weighs 50 pounds.

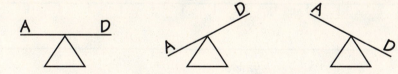

Use the diagram to help you solve the problems.

1. Abe and Dee get on the see-saw. Circle what it looks like.

2. Foy gets on with Abe. Draw what the see-saw looks like.

3. Who can get on with Cy so that the see-saw balances? _____

MONTHLY ASSESSMENT

1. Name five ways to make 37¢. You have quarters, dimes, nickels, and pennies. You must use at least three different kinds of coins.

   _____

2. Look at the figures. Think of a way to sort all the figures into two categories. What are the categories?

   _____

   _____

   _____

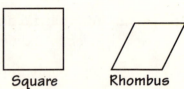

Square   Rhombus

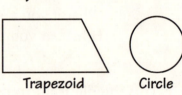

Trapezoid   Circle

3. Which figures fit into each of your categories?

   _____

   _____

   _____

4. Now think of a way to sort all of these figures into three categories.

   What are the categories? _____

   _____

5. Which figures fit into each of these new categories? _____

   _____

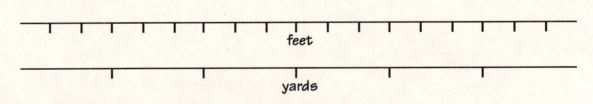

feet

yards

Use the diagram to help you solve the problems.

6. How many feet are in $5\frac{1}{3}$ yards? _____ feet

7. How many full yards are in 14 feet? _____

8. How many extra feet? _____

9. Write a mixed number to tell the number of yards in 22 feet. _____

DAY 1

Use the Counting Tape. Give just the remainder for each division problem.

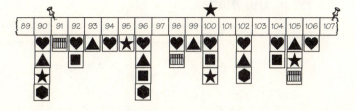

1. 97 ÷ 2 The remainder is _____

2. 97 ÷ 3 The remainder is _____

3. 97 ÷ 4 The remainder is _____

4. 97 ÷ 5 The remainder is _____

5. 97 ÷ 6 The remainder is _____

_____ _____ _____

6. Describe the pattern using letters. _____

7. Describe the pattern using numbers. _____

DAY 2

1. Which of these numbers are factors of 100? 1, 2, 3, 4, 5, 6, 7.

_____

Number	How many 5's?
5	1
10	2
15	3
20	4
25	5

2. How many 5's will be in 50? _____

3. How many 5's will be in 60? _____

4. How many 5's will be in 80? _____

5. How many 5's will be in 100? _____

6. How do you know? _____

Use the diagram to help you fill in the blanks.

7. $\frac{3}{16}$ lb = _____ oz

8. 6 oz = _____ lb or _____ lb

9. Find a number of ounces that you can write as pounds in 3 different ways. _____

DAY 3

Fill in the blanks.

1. $2 \times 3 =$ _____   2. $3 \times 3 =$ _____   3. $4 \times 3 =$ _____   4. $5 \times 3 =$ _____

   $2 \times 6 =$ _____ $3 \times 6 =$ _____ $4 \times 6 =$ _____ $5 \times 6 =$ _____

5. $6 \times 3 =$ _____   6. $7 \times 3 =$ _____   7. $8 \times 3 =$ _____   8. $9 \times 3 =$ _____

   $6 \times 6 =$ _____ $7 \times 6 =$ _____ $8 \times 6 =$ _____ $9 \times 6 =$ _____

9. Compare multiplying a number by 3 and multiplying it by 6. _____

   _____

10. Compare the figures. Tell two ways that the figures are different.

    _____

    _____

11. Tell one way that the figures are the same. _____

    _____

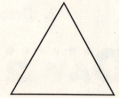

DAY 4

Fill in the blanks.

1. $(2 \times 7) + (1 \times 7) = 3 \times 7$

   _____ + _____ = _____

2. $(2 \times 7) + (2 \times 7) = 4 \times 7$

   _____ + _____ = _____

3. $(2 \times 7) + (3 \times 7) = 5 \times 7$

   _____ + _____ = _____

4. $(2 \times 7) + (4 \times 7) = 6 \times 7$

   _____ + _____ = _____

5. Suzanna goes to camp every summer.
   She spends 2 weeks at tennis camp,
   1 week at art camp and 3 weeks
   at sleep-away camp. How many days
   is Suzanna at camp altogether?   _____

DAY 5

Write 2 or 3 in the blanks to make the equations true.

1. _____ × 27 = 54   2. _____ × 20 = 60

3. _____ × 6 = 18   4. _____ × 25 = 50

5. _____ × 10 = 30   6. _____ × 7 = 21

7. _____ × 29 = 58   8. _____ × 9 = 18

9. _____ × 9 = 27   10. _____ × 17 = 34

11. I am thinking of a number:
   • It is even
   • It has a remainder of 1 when divided by 3
   • It has a remainder of 2 when divided by 4
   • It has a remainder of 4 when divided by 5
   • It is one day less than 5 weeks

   What is my number and how do you know? _____

   _____

DAY 6

Multiply mentally.

1. 3 × 100 = _____   2. 4 × 100 = _____

3. 13 × 100 = _____   4. 14 × 100 = _____

5. 23 × 100 = _____   6. 24 × 100 = _____

7. 30 × 100 = _____   8. 40 × 100 = _____

9. What do you notice about the factors and products when you multiply by 100?

   _____

   _____

   _____

Complete the pattern.

10. 10, 20, 30, 100, 200, 300, _____, _____, _____, _____, _____, 30,000

DAY 7

Write 10 or 100 in the blanks to make the equations true.

1. _____ × 30 = 300

2. _____ × 16 = 160

3. _____ × 20 = 2000

4. _____ × 6 = 60

5. _____ × 27 = 2700

6. _____ × 28 = 2800

7. If you multiply the same number by 10 and by 100, how are the products different?

_____

_____

_____

8. If you have three nickels and one dime, what additional coin do you need to give you $0.35? Draw a ring around the coin.

9. If you have one quarter, two dimes and one nickel, what additional coin do you need to give you $0.75? Draw a ring around the coin.

DAY 8

Write 4, 5, or 6 in the blanks to make the equations true.

1. 12 ÷ _____ = 2

2. 15 ÷ _____ = 3

3. 16 ÷ _____ = 4

4. 18 ÷ 3 = _____

5. 20 ÷ _____ = 4

6. 24 ÷ _____ = 6

7. 20 ÷ _____ = 5

8. 24 ÷ _____ = 6

9. 30 ÷ _____ = 6

10. 25 ÷ _____ = 5

11. 30 ÷ _____ = 5

12. 28 ÷ _____ = 7

13. 12 ÷ 3 = _____

14. 36 ÷ _____ = 6

15. 32 ÷ 8 = _____

16. 35 ÷ 7 = _____

17. 48 ÷ _____ = 8

18. 40 ÷ 8 = _____

 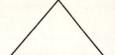 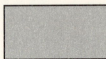

19. Tell how each of the figures is different from the other. _____

_____

DAY 9

3	7	35	15	24		6	
100	4	21	30	42	**20**	5	

Use only these numbers to solve the problems. You may use a number twice.

1. Write at least 4 multiplication equations. _____

   _____

2. Write at least 4 division equations. _____

   _____

3. Arnell is in charge of the community dinner. She must tell the cooks to the closest 10 how many people will be eating. What would be her answer if 257 people said they were coming? _____

DAY 10   CHECKPOINT

Use the numbers 1 through 50. Write eight multiplication or division equations in which one number is 4, 5, 6 or 7.

1. _____   2. _____

3. _____   4. _____

5. _____   6. _____

7. _____   8. _____

Write the remainders.

9. $86 \div 2 = 43$ R_____   10. $86 \div 3 = 28$ R_____   11. $86 \div 4 = 21$ R_____

12. $86 \div 5 = 17$ R_____   13. $86 \div 6 = 14$ R_____   14. $86 \div 10 = 8$ R_____

15. Which two remainders in problems 9 through 14 were easiest to figure out? Why?

   _____

   _____

Fill in the blanks.

16. $10 \times 40 =$ _____   17. $100 \times 32 =$ _____   18. $100 \times 30 =$ _____

DAY 11

Round these numbers to the nearest ten.

1. 58 rounds to _____
2. 115 rounds to _____
3. 73 rounds to _____
4. 137 rounds to _____
5. 98 rounds to _____
6. 363 rounds to _____

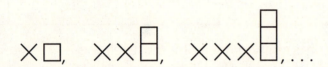

7. Draw the 9th figure in this pattern.

8. How did you get your answer? _____

_____

_____

_____

DAY 12

Round these numbers to the nearest hundred.

1. 156 rounds to _____
2. 627 rounds to _____
3. 223 rounds to _____
4. 989 rounds to _____
5. 777 rounds to _____
6. 453 rounds to _____

7. At the orange juice festival contest, Team A squeezed 14 cups of orange juice, Team B squeezed 16 cups, and Team C squeezed 15 cups. How many quarts did each team squeeze?

_____

_____

_____

DAY 13

Round these numbers to the nearest thousand.

1. 2756 rounds to _____

2. 9009 rounds to _____

3. 5122 rounds to _____

4. 12,892 rounds to _____

5. 7507 rounds to _____

6. 13,121 rounds to _____

7. Sort the figures into two categories. What is your rule for each category and

which figures go in each? _____

_____

8. Sort the figures into two different categories. What is your rule for each category

and which figures go in each? _____

_____

DAY 14

Fill in this table by rounding the number in each row to the place in each column.

		round to 10's	round to 100's	round to 1000's
1.	7526			
2.	9075			
3.	8657			

Fill in the blanks using some of the numbers in the box. Be sure the paragraph
makes sense.

16	2000	90	98,632	3229	27
6224		126,285		14	
17,623	10,000	29,346	2	500	79

4. There were _____ people at the professional football game. _____ soft drinks

were sold and _____ hot dogs. _____ people each won a door prize of $_____,

not nearly enough to buy a car, but enough for a nice sound system. The score was

_____ for the winner and _____ for the loser.

DAY 15

Match the numbers to the expanded notation (not all can be matched).

1. 1075

   a. 3000 + 200 + 60 + 8

   b. 1000 + 70 + 5

2. 3268

   c. 30,000 + 2000 + 60 + 8

   d. 100,000 + 90,000 + 900 + 1

3. 19,091

   e. 6000 + 600 + 20 + 1

   f. 10,000 + 9000 + 90 + 1

4. 65,620

   g. 60,000 + 5000 + 600 + 20

5. At the state fair, you get twelve counters to place on the circle. Your opponent also gets twelve. Each counter is valued by its placement on the circle. The object is to use all twelve and get as close as you can to 1,000,000 without going over. Where would you place the remaining three counters?

   _____

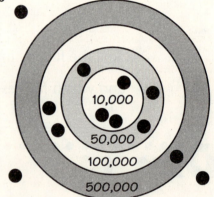

DAY 16

Write 7, 2, 10, or 20 in the blanks to make the equations true.

1. 240 = 12 × _____

2. 100 × _____ = 200

3. 70 ÷ _____ = 7

4. 210 ÷ 30 = _____

5. 140 ÷ 20 = _____

6. 400 × _____ = 2800

7. 700 ÷ 100 = _____

8. 630 ÷ 90 = _____

9. 70 × _____ = 490

10. 350 ÷ 50 = _____

11. 600 × _____ = 4200

12. 70 × _____ = 140

Complete the patterns.

13. 35, 28, _____, _____, _____, 0.

14. 1, 8, 15, 22, _____, _____, _____, _____, 57.

DAY 17

Fill in the blanks.

1. 36 ÷ 7 = _____ remainder _____
2. 35 ÷ 6 = _____ remainder _____
3. 42 ÷ 7 = _____ remainder _____
4. 42 ÷ 6 = _____ remainder _____
5. 50 ÷ 7 = _____ remainder _____
6. 50 ÷ 6 = _____ remainder _____
7. 66 ÷ 7 = _____ remainder _____
8. 60 ÷ 6 = _____ remainder _____

9. 18 ounces = _____ pounds
10. 19 ounces = _____
11. 20 ounces = _____
12. 21 ounces = _____
13. 22 ounces = _____
14. 23 ounces = _____
15. 30 ounces = _____
16. 32 ounces = _____

DAY 18

Solve mentally.

1. 24 ÷ _____ = 8
2. 16 ÷ _____ = 8
3. 20 ÷ 5 = _____
4. 18 ÷ 3 = _____
5. 36 ÷ 4 = _____
6. 28 ÷ _____ = 4
7. 36 ÷ 6 = _____
8. 35 ÷ 7 = _____
9. 16 ÷ 4 = _____
10. 45 ÷ 5 = _____
11. 48 ÷ 6 = _____
12. 12 ÷ 4 = _____
13. 40 ÷ 8 = _____
14. 56 ÷ _____ = 7
15. 42 ÷ 6 = _____

16. Sort the figures into two categories. What is your rule for each category and which figures go in each?

   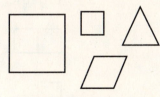

   _____

   _____

17. Sort the figures into three different categories. What is your rule for each category and which figures go in each?

   _____

   _____

DAY 19

Subtract mentally.

1. 700 − 119 = _____

2. 925 − 230 = _____

3. 991 − 181 = _____

4. 650 − 125 = _____

5. 723 − 625 = _____

6. 457 − 123 = _____

7. Alan scored 97, 93, 95 on his spelling tests.
   What is Alan's average spelling grade? _____

DAY 20

Subtract mentally.

1. 1000 − 200 = _____

2. 12,000 − 150 = _____

3. 17,600 − 1500 = _____

4. 1100 − 100 = _____

5. 13,500 − 450 = _____

6. 18,000 − 900 = _____

7. 1100 − 200 = _____

8. 14,300 − 1200 = _____

You are playing a game.

- The game pieces are

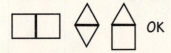

- The rules say you must put the pieces
  together so that 2 sides match exactly.

OK

NOT OK

- Your score is the perimeter of your construction.

9. Show how you could reach a goal of 14 points.
   How many triangles and squares did you use? _____

1	2	3	4	5	6	7	8	9	10
11	12	13	14	15	16	17	18	19	20
21	22	23	24	25	26	27	28	29	30
31	32	33	34	35	36	37	38	39	40
41	42	43	44	45	46	47	48	49	50
51	52	53	54	55	56	57	58	59	60
61	62	63	64	65	66	67	68	69	70
71	72	73	74	75	76	77	78	79	80
81	82	83	84	85	86	87	88	89	90
91	92	93	94	95	96	97	98	99	100

Use the Hundred Chart.

1. Shade in both diagonals. What do you notice about the numbers in the 1 to 100 diagonal? _____

    _____

    _____

2. What do you notice about the numbers in the 10 to 91 diagonal? _____

    _____

    _____

3. How are the patterns in the two diagonals the same? _____

    _____

    _____

4. How are the patterns in the two diagonals different? _____

    _____

    _____

MONTHLY ASSESSMENT

Use the Counting Tape.

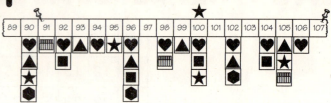

1. 97 ÷ 2 The remainder is _____

2. 97 ÷ 3 The remainder is _____

3. 97 ÷ 4 The remainder is _____   4. 97 ÷ 5 The remainder is _____

5. 97 ÷ 6 The remainder is _____   6. 97 ÷ 7 The remainder is _____

Fill in the blanks.

7. 8 × 3 = _____   8. 7 × 3 = _____   9. _____ × 3 = 27

   8 × _____ = 48   7 × _____ = 42   9 × 6 = _____

10. 4 × 10 = _____   11. 6 × 10 = _____   12. 15 × 10 = _____

    4 × 20 = _____   6 × _____ = 120   15 × 20 = _____

13. 4 × 100 = _____   14. 14 × 100 = _____   15. _____ × 100 = 2400

Write 2, 3, or 10 in the blanks to make the equations true.

16. _____ × 26 = 52   17. 30 × _____ = 300   18. 84 ÷ _____ = 28

19. 24 ÷ _____ = 8   20. 480 ÷ _____ = 48   21. _____ × 18 = 36

Use the number 12,608 to solve the problems.

22. Round to the nearest 10. _____

23. Round to the nearest 100. _____

24. Add 5000 and round to the nearest 1000. _____

Write in expanded notation.

25. 765 _____   26. 7605 _____

27. 70,650 _____

Subtract mentally.

28. 2000 − 800 = _____   29. 14,000 − 250 = _____

30. 19,200 − 1200 = _____

A

B

C

Use these coins to solve the problems.

1. What one coin makes A and B equal? What row would you put it in?

   _____

2. Draw coins in row C so that the sum of all the money in rows A, B, and C is $1.00.

3. You can buy juice boxes in packs of 2, 4, or 6. Write two ways you can buy exactly fourteen juice boxes. _____

4. Can you buy exactly thirty-five juice boxes? Explain. _____

   _____

Get a coin or a counter with faces marked *heads* and *tails*.

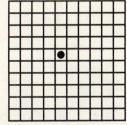

- Start with your pencil on the dot and move one space in any direction.

- Flip your coin. Heads means turn right and move one space. Tails means turn left and move 1 space.

5. Predict whether you will get back to the dot or go off the grid first.

   _____

6. Flip the coin five times. Do you want to change your prediction from problem 5?

   _____

   _____

7. Flip the coin five more times. Do you want to change your prediction? Explain.

   _____

   _____

MONTHLY ASSESSMENT

You are playing a game.

A. The game pieces are

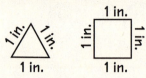

B. The rules say you must put the pieces together so 2 sides match exactly.

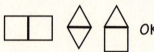

OK

C. Your score is the perimeter of your construction.

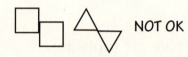

NOT OK

1. Show how you could reach a goal of twenty points using some of each kind of piece.

2. Show how you could reach a goal of twenty points using only one kind of piece.

3. Show two ways to write six ounces as a fraction of a pound. _____

4. Find all the numbers of ounces you can only write as a fraction in one way.

_____

5. What do you notice about these numbers? _____

_____

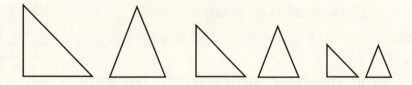

6. Compare the figures. How are these figures alike? _____

_____

7. Sort all the figures into two categories. What are the rules for your categories and

   what figures are in them? _____

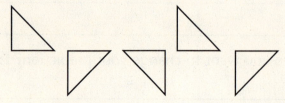

8. Study the pattern. Draw the sixth and seventh figures.

Fill in the blanks. Use each product to find the next one.

1. $1 \times 2 =$ _____

      _____ $\times 2 =$ _____

          _____ $\times 2 =$ _____ and $1 \times 8 =$ _____

2. $2 \times 2 =$ _____

      _____ $\times 2 =$ _____

          _____ $\times 2 =$ _____ and $2 \times 8 =$ _____

3. $3 \times 2 =$ _____

      _____ $\times 2 =$ _____

          _____ $\times 2 =$ _____ and $3 \times 8 =$ _____

Complete the patterns.

4. 0, 4, 8, _____, 40

5. 0, 8, 16, 24, 32, _____, 56, 64, 72, _____

DAY 2

Use the numbers 6 or 7 to fill in the blanks.

1. $6 \times$ _____ $= 36$ **2.** $42 \div 6 =$ _____   **3.** $56 \div 8 =$ _____

4. $21 \div$ _____ $= 3$ **5.** $30 \div 5 =$ _____   **6.** $9 \times$ _____ $= 63$

7. $35 \div 5 =$ _____   **8.** $8 \times$ _____ $= 48$ **9.** $49 \div 7 =$ _____

Fill in the blanks with whole numbers, fractions, or mixed numbers.

10. $16 \text{ oz} =$ _____ lb   **11.** $32 \text{ oz} =$ _____ lb

12. $8 \text{ oz} =$ _____ lb   **13.** $24 \text{ oz} =$ _____ lb

14. $48 \text{ oz} =$ _____ lb   **15.** $4 \text{ oz} =$ _____ lb

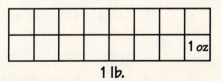

1 lb.

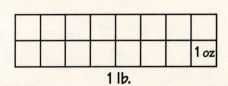

1 lb.

DAY 3

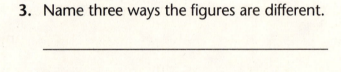

8   **40**   32   36   *6*   **24**   30   3
4   18   2   20   5   **7**   9   28   **42**

1. Use these numbers to write at least eight equations. You may use numbers more

   than once. _____

   _____

2. Name three ways the figures are alike.

   _____

   _____

   _____

3. Name three ways the figures are different.

   _____

   _____

   _____

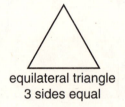

equilateral triangle
3 sides equal

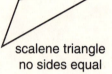

scalene triangle
no sides equal

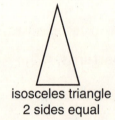

isosceles triangle
2 sides equal

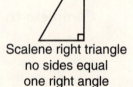

Scalene right triangle
no sides equal
one right angle

DAY 4

Use the Counting Tape.

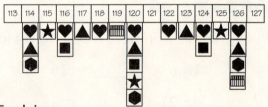

1. What factors of 120 are shown?

   1, _____ 120

2. Do you think there are other factors of 120? Explain.

   _____

3. What numbers in the tape have 2 and 3 as common factors? _____

   _____

4. Do the numbers that have 2 and 3 as common factors also have 6 as a factor?

   Explain. _____

   _____

5. Jordan spent $0.59 at the store. He started
   with $5.00. How much change did he receive? _____

DAY 5

Help Mrs. Cooke correct this test by finding the wrong answers and correcting them.

1. $\begin{array}{r} 7 \\ \times\,3 \\ \hline 21 \end{array}$
2. $\begin{array}{r} 7 \\ \times\,6 \\ \hline 43 \end{array}$
3. $\begin{array}{r} 6 \\ \times\,6 \\ \hline 36 \end{array}$
4. $\begin{array}{r} 7 \\ \times\,5 \\ \hline 35 \end{array}$
5. $\begin{array}{r} 7 \\ \times\,8 \\ \hline 65 \end{array}$

6. $17 \div 3 = 5 \text{ R2}$

7. $17 \div 4 = 4 \text{ R2}$

8. $17 \div 8 = 1 \text{ R7}$

9. $27 \div 3 = 9$

10. $27 \div 4 = 8$

11. $27 \div 8 = 4 \text{ R3}$

12. $10 \times 70 = 7000$

13. $20 \times 70 = 1400$

14. Alton invited friends over to play games. He invited six friends. Can they all play games involving two children and games involving four children without anyone being left out? Explain. _____

_____

_____

15. How many more friends could Alton invite so that no one would be left out? Explain. _____

_____

DAY 6

Solve mentally.

1. $\begin{array}{r} 760 \\ +\,323 \end{array}$
2. $\begin{array}{r} 1083 \\ -\,323 \end{array}$
3. $\begin{array}{r} 952 \\ +\,447 \end{array}$
4. $\begin{array}{r} 1399 \\ -\,447 \end{array}$
5. $\begin{array}{r} 851 \\ +\,537 \end{array}$
6. $\begin{array}{r} 1388 \\ -\,537 \end{array}$

Complete the patterns.

7. 0, 7, 14, _____, 63

8. 1, 8, 15, 22, _____, 57

9. 2, 10, 18, 26, _____, 74

DAY 7

Write these numbers in expanded notation.

1. 121,527 _____

2. 310,607 _____

3. 905,555 _____

4. Tell what time it will be 28 minutes from now.	5. Tell what time it was 50 minutes ago.	6. Tell what time it will be 50 minutes from now.
_____	_____	_____

DAY 8

Round to the place indicated.

1. $106,227 to the nearest hundred _____

2. $106,527 to the nearest hundred _____

3. $106,527 to the nearest thousand _____

4. $110,727 to the nearest hundred _____

5. $110,727 to the nearest thousand _____

6. $121,527 to the nearest hundred _____

7. $121,527 to the nearest thousand _____

8. $121,527 to the nearest ten-thousand _____

9. An equilateral triangle has _____ equal sides.

10. An isosceles triangle has _____ equal sides.

11. Tell two ways isosceles and equilateral triangles are alike. _____

_____

DAY 9

For problems 1 through 5, use this number: 121,527.

1. What would the number be if it were 2 less? _____

2. What would the number be if it were 70 more? _____

3. What would the number be if it were 8,000 more? _____

4. What would the number be if it were 10,000 less? _____

5. What would the number be if it were 100,000 less? _____

6. Ananda went to the grocery store. She had $10.00 and got $8.76 in change. How much money did Ananda spend? _____

DAY 10   CHECKPOINT

Fill in the blanks.

1. _____ × 6 = 18   2. _____ × 8 = 32   3. _____ × 7 = 21

4. 10 × 70 = _____   5. _____ × 70 = 1400   6. 20 × _____ = 140

Use the graph to fill in the blanks.

7. _____ more people chose pizza than chose hamburgers.

8. _____ more people chose pizza than chose chicken.

9. _____ more people chose hamburgers than chose chicken.

Round $176,827 to the place indicated.

10. Round to the nearest 100. _____   11. Round to the nearest 10,000. _____

Fill in the blanks.

12. 10 oz = _____ lb   13. 5 oz = _____ lb   14. 5 lb = _____ oz

Solve mentally.

15.   743   16.   869   17.   452   18.   1273
    + 126   − 126   + 821   − 821

DAY 11

Fill in the blanks to make the equations true.

1. (_____ × 8) + (_____ × 8) = 8

2. (_____ × 8) + (_____ × 8) = 16

3. (_____ × 8) + (_____ × 8) = 24

4. (_____ × 8) + (_____ × 8) = 32

Complete the pattern.

5. 1, 4, 3, 6, 5, 8, 7, _____, 14.

6. Describe the rule for your pattern. _____

_____

_____

_____

_____

DAY 12

Fill in the blanks to make the equations true.

1. (_____ × 8) + (_____ × 8) = 72

2. (_____ × 8) + (_____ × 8) = 64

3. (_____ × 8) + (_____ × 8) = 56

4. (_____ × 8) + (_____ × 8) = 48

Fill in the blanks.

5. 1 meter = _____ centimeters

6. 90 centimeters = _____ meter or _____ meter

7. 0.6 meter = _____ centimeters

8. 1.2 meters = _____ centimeters

DAY 13

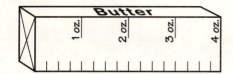

Use the diagram to help you fill in the blanks.

1. $\frac{1}{4}$ stick of butter = _____ ounce

2. $\frac{1}{2}$ stick of butter = _____

3. $\frac{1}{8}$ stick of butter = _____

4. $\frac{1}{16}$ stick of butter = _____

5. Which of these triangles has a line of

   symmetry? Draw the lines. _____

   _____

   _____

equilateral triangle

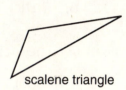

scalene triangle

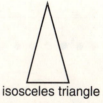

isosceles triangle

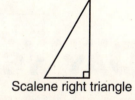

Scalene right triangle

DAY 14

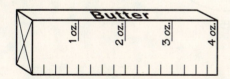

Use the diagram to help you fill in the blanks.

1. $\frac{1}{2}$ stick of butter + $\frac{1}{2}$ stick of butter = _____ stick of butter.

2. $\frac{1}{2}$ stick of butter + $\frac{1}{4}$ stick of butter = _____ stick of butter.

3. $\frac{1}{2}$ stick of butter + $\frac{1}{8}$ stick of butter = _____ stick of butter.

4. $\frac{1}{2}$ stick of butter + $\frac{1}{16}$ stick of butter = _____ stick of butter.

5. Jamell got $\frac{1}{2}$ of the puzzle put together, and Ed added $\frac{1}{4}$
   more. How much of the puzzle is left to be put together? _____

DAY 15

Use the diagram to help you fill in the blanks.

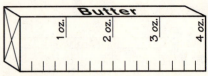

1. $\frac{1}{4}$ stick of butter + $\frac{1}{4}$ stick of butter = _____ stick of butter

2. $\frac{1}{4}$ stick of butter + $\frac{1}{8}$ stick of butter = _____ stick of butter

3. $\frac{1}{8}$ stick of butter + $\frac{1}{8}$ stick of butter = _____ stick of butter

4. $\frac{1}{2}$ stick of butter + $\frac{1}{8}$ stick of butter = _____ stick of butter

5. $\frac{1}{4}$ stick of butter + $\frac{1}{16}$ stick of butter = _____ stick of butter

6. $\frac{1}{8}$ stick of butter + $\frac{1}{8}$ stick of butter + $\frac{1}{8}$ stick of butter = _____ stick of butter

7. The factors of my number are: 1, 2, 5, 10, 25, and 50. What is my number? Write

   about how you know the answer. _____

   _____

DAY 16

A

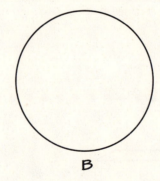

B

1. How many pennies are in circle A? _____

2. If you put half the pennies in circle B, how many pennies would be in circle B? _____

3. If you put $\frac{1}{4}$ of the pennies in circle B, how many would be in circle B? _____

4. If you put $\frac{1}{4}$ of the pennies in circle B, how many are left in circle A? _____

5. If you put $\frac{1}{3}$ of the pennies in circle B, how many would be in circle B? _____

6. If you put $\frac{2}{4}$ of the pennies in circle B, how many would be in circle B? _____

Complete the patterns.

7. $\frac{1}{2}$, $\frac{2}{4}$, $\frac{3}{6}$, _____, $\frac{10}{20}$

8. $\frac{1}{4}$, $\frac{2}{8}$, $\frac{3}{12}$, $\frac{4}{16}$, _____, $\frac{10}{40}$.

DAY 17

1. How many pennies in the whole bunch of pennies? _____

2. How many pennies in $\frac{1}{2}$ of the bunch? _____

3. How many pennies in $\frac{1}{4}$ of the bunch? _____

4. How many pennies in $\frac{1}{5}$ of the bunch? _____

5. How many pennies in $\frac{1}{10}$ of the bunch? _____

6. How many centimeters are in $\frac{1}{2}$ of a meter? _____

7. How many centimeters are in $\frac{1}{4}$ of a meter? _____

8. How many centimeters are in $\frac{1}{5}$ of a meter? _____

9. How many centimeters are in $\frac{1}{10}$ of a meter? _____

10. How many centimeters are in $\frac{1}{20}$ of a meter? _____

11. How many centimeters are in 2 meters? _____

DAY 18

1 whole, or 1 yard			1 whole, or 1 yard			1 whole, or 1 yard			1 whole, or 1 yard			1 whole, or 1 yard			1 whole, or 1 yard			1 whole, or 1 yard			1 whole, or 1 yard		
1 ft ($\frac{1}{3}$ yd)	1 ft ($\frac{1}{3}$ yd)	1 ft ($\frac{1}{3}$ yd)	1 ft ($\frac{1}{3}$ yd)	1 ft ($\frac{1}{3}$ yd)	1 ft ($\frac{1}{3}$ yd)	1 ft ($\frac{1}{3}$ yd)	1 ft ($\frac{1}{3}$ yd)	1 ft ($\frac{1}{3}$ yd)	1 ft ($\frac{1}{3}$ yd)	1 ft ($\frac{1}{3}$ yd)	1 ft ($\frac{1}{3}$ yd)	1 ft ($\frac{1}{3}$ yd)	1 ft ($\frac{1}{3}$ yd)	1 ft ($\frac{1}{3}$ yd)	1 ft ($\frac{1}{3}$ yd)	1 ft ($\frac{1}{3}$ yd)	1 ft ($\frac{1}{3}$ yd)	1 ft ($\frac{1}{3}$ yd)	1 ft ($\frac{1}{3}$ yd)	1 ft ($\frac{1}{3}$ yd)	1 ft ($\frac{1}{3}$ yd)	1 ft ($\frac{1}{3}$ yd)	1 ft ($\frac{1}{3}$ yd)

Use the diagram.

1. 1 whole yard = _____ feet

2. $\frac{1}{3}$ yard = _____

3. $\frac{2}{3}$ yard = _____

4. $1\frac{1}{3}$ yards = _____

5. $1\frac{2}{3}$ yards = _____

6. 2 yards = _____

7. $2\frac{1}{3}$ yards = _____

8. $2\frac{2}{3}$ yards = _____

9. 3 yards = _____

10. Are these triangles the same? If so, what has happened to them? If not, explain

how you know. _____

_____

DAY 19

Fill in the blanks.

1. 1 whole hour = _____ minutes

2. $\frac{1}{2}$ hour = _____

3. $\frac{1}{4}$ hour = _____

4. $\frac{1}{6}$ hour = _____

5. $\frac{1}{10}$ hour = _____

6. $\frac{1}{12}$ hour = _____

7. $1\frac{1}{4}$ hours = _____

8. $1\frac{1}{12}$ hours = _____

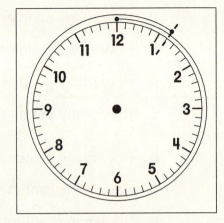

66 minutes = 1 hour
and six minutes

9. Brandon has a project due on March 18. If he does $\frac{1}{8}$ of the work each night, how much should he have done at the end of 6 nights? _____

10. How much of the work will he have left? _____

11. How much longer will it take him to finish it? _____

DAY 20

Use the diagram.

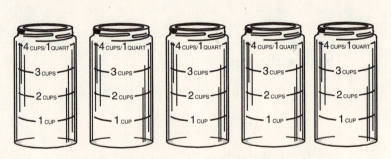

1. 1 whole quart = _____ cups

2. $\frac{1}{2}$ quart = _____

3. $\frac{1}{4}$ quart = _____

4. $1\frac{1}{2}$ quarts = _____   5. 2 quarts = _____

6. 17 cups = _____   7. 18 cups = _____

8. 19 cups = _____   9. 20 cups = _____

10. Paloma has to add four quarts of water to some lemon juice to make lemonade. She has one cup and a small jar with which to measure. How can Paloma use both the cup and the jar to measure four quarts?

_____

_____

MONTHLY ASSESSMENT

1. What figures make up the pattern? _____

   _____

2. Use words to describe the pattern of triangles.

   _____

3. Use letters to describe the light and dark pattern

   of the shading. _____

   _____

4. There are 31 days in March. Continue the
   pattern through the rest of the month.

5. Write three sentences describing other things you see in the calendar patterns.

   _____

   _____

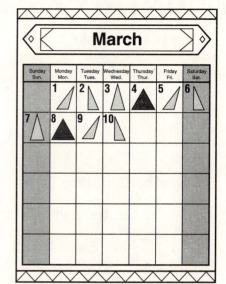

6. Make up a shape pattern and fill in the month.

7. Describe your shape pattern. _____

   _____

   _____

MONTHLY ASSESSMENT

Fill in the blanks.

1. 6 × 7 = _____

2. 8 × _____ = 56

3. _____ × 7 = 35

4. 17 ÷ 4 = 4 R_____

5. 37 ÷ 6 = _____

6. 100 × _____ = 7000

7. If 156 + 38 = 194, then 194 − 38 = _____

Use the Counting Tape.

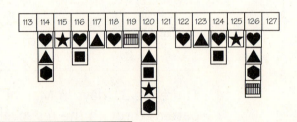

8. List the numbers that have 2 as a factor.

_____

9. List the numbers that have 5 as a factor. _____

_____

10. Predict another factor that you should see any number with both 2 and 5 as factors. _____

Write the numbers in expanded notation.

11. 40,006 _____

12. 40,060 _____

Round to the indicated place.

13. $145,621 to the nearest hundred is _____

14. $145,621 to the nearest thousand is _____

15. $145,621 to the nearest ten-thousand is _____

Problems 16 through 18 ask about the number 132,055.

16. What would the number be if it were 50 more? _____

17. What would the number be if it were 500 more? _____

18. What would the number be if it were 5000 more? _____

Fill in the blanks to make the equations true.

19. (_____ × 8) + (_____ × 8) = 40

20. (_____ × 5) + (_____ × 5) = 45

MONTHLY ASSESSMENT

1. This shows the money Renee has. She wants to buy a burger for $4.25. The clerk is out of coins. What should Renee give the clerk and what change should she get?

   _____ _____

2. How much more money does Renee need to have $10? _____

3. The soda machine takes dollar bills and coins. What coins would Renee use to buy a soda for 75¢ and what change would she get?

   _____

4. Is there another way to solve problem 3? _____

   _____

A   B   C   D

5. If float A must go first, show the ways the floats could line up for the parade.

   _____

6. How do you know you have found all the possible ways? _____

   _____

7. Predict the number of ways to line up the floats if float B has to go first. Explain

   your prediction. _____

   _____

8. This is a school building with a lining-up place in the school yard. Show what you think the fire drill routes and line-up positions should be for each classroom. Write an explanation of a fire drill procedure for room 11.

   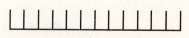

   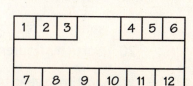

   _____

   _____

MONTHLY ASSESSMENT

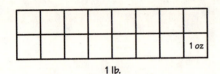

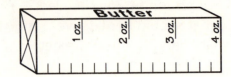

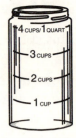

1 whole, or 1 yard			1 whole, or 1 yard			1 whole, or 1 yard			1 whole, or 1 yard			1 whole, or 1 yard			1 whole, or 1 yard			1 whole, or 1 yard			1 whole, or 1 yard		
1 ft ($\frac{1}{3}$ yd)	1 ft ($\frac{1}{3}$ yd)	1 ft ($\frac{1}{3}$ yd)	1 ft ($\frac{1}{3}$ yd)	1 ft ($\frac{1}{3}$ yd)	1 ft ($\frac{1}{3}$ yd)	1 ft ($\frac{1}{3}$ yd)	1 ft ($\frac{1}{3}$ yd)	1 ft ($\frac{1}{3}$ yd)	1 ft ($\frac{1}{3}$ yd)	1 ft ($\frac{1}{3}$ yd)	1 ft ($\frac{1}{3}$ yd)	1 ft ($\frac{1}{3}$ yd)	1 ft ($\frac{1}{3}$ yd)	1 ft ($\frac{1}{3}$ yd)	1 ft ($\frac{1}{3}$ yd)	1 ft ($\frac{1}{3}$ yd)	1 ft ($\frac{1}{3}$ yd)	1 ft ($\frac{1}{3}$ yd)	1 ft ($\frac{1}{3}$ yd)	1 ft ($\frac{1}{3}$ yd)	1 ft ($\frac{1}{3}$ yd)	1 ft ($\frac{1}{3}$ yd)	1 ft ($\frac{1}{3}$ yd)

Use the diagrams to help you fill in the blanks.

1. $4\frac{1}{2}$ quarts = _____

2. $\frac{1}{4}$ stick of butter = _____ ounce

3. $\frac{5}{8}$ lb = _____

4. 14 oz = _____

5. $3\frac{2}{3}$ yards = _____

6. 2 quarts = _____

7. 6 oz = _____

8. $\frac{1}{2}$ stick of butter = _____ ounces

9. $2\frac{1}{3}$ yards = _____

10. 8 feet = _____

11. 15 cups = _____

12. 32 oz = _____

13. $\frac{1}{2}$ stick of butter + $\frac{1}{2}$ stick of butter = _____ ounces

14. $\frac{1}{4}$ stick of butter + $\frac{1}{4}$ stick of butter + $\frac{1}{4}$ stick of butter = _____ ounces

Fill in the blanks.

15. 800 centimeters = _____ meters

16. 2 meters = _____ centimeters

17. 1.3 meters = _____

18. 600 centimeters = _____

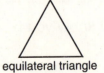
equilateral triangle

scalene triangle

isosceles triangle

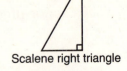
Scalene right triangle

19. Sort the figures into two categories. Give the rules for your categories and tell what figures are in each. _____

_____

20. Sort the figures into two different categories. Give the rules for your categories and tell what figures are in each. _____

DAY 1 • APRIL

Fill in the blanks. Use each product to find the next one.

1. $1 \times 3 =$ _____
   ↓
   _____ $\times 3 =$ _____ and $1 \times 9 =$ _____

2. $2 \times 3 =$ _____
   ↓
   _____ $\times 3 =$ _____ and $2 \times 9 =$ _____

3. $3 \times 3 =$ _____
   ↓
   _____ $\times 3 =$ _____ and $3 \times 9 =$ _____

Complete the patterns.

4. 80, 72, 64, 56, _____, 0.

5. 0, 9, 18, 27, _____, 90.

DAY 2 •

Fill in the blanks. Use each product to find the next one.

1. $5 \times 3 =$ _____
   ↓
   _____ $\times 3 =$ _____ and $5 \times 9 =$ _____

2. $6 \times 3 =$ _____
   ↓
   _____ $\times 3 =$ _____ and $6 \times 9 =$ _____

Fill in the blanks.

3. $\frac{1}{2}$ meter = _____ centimeters
4. 150 centimeters = 1.5 _____

5. $\frac{1}{4}$ meter = _____ centimeters
6. 131 centimeters = _____ meters

Fill in the blanks.

7. $\frac{1}{2}$ dollar = _____ pennies or $_____

8. $\frac{1}{4}$ dollar = _____ pennies or $_____

9. $\frac{1}{5}$ dollar = _____ pennies or _____

10. $\frac{1}{10}$ dollar = _____ pennies or _____

DAY 3

Fill in the blanks. Remember: always work inside the parentheses first.

1. $(1 \times 8) + (\underline{\hspace{1cm}} \times 8) = 8$ $8 = 8 \times (1 + \underline{\hspace{1cm}})$

2. $(1 \times 8) + (\underline{\hspace{1cm}} \times 8) = 16$ $16 = 8 \times (\underline{\hspace{1cm}} + \underline{\hspace{1cm}})$

3. $(2 \times 8) + (\underline{\hspace{1cm}} \times 8) = 24$ $24 = 8 \times (\underline{\hspace{1cm}} + \underline{\hspace{1cm}})$

4. $(2 \times 8) + (\underline{\hspace{1cm}} \times 8) = 32$ $32 = 8 \times (\underline{\hspace{1cm}} + \underline{\hspace{1cm}})$

5. $(2 \times 8) + (\underline{\hspace{1cm}} \times 8) = 40$ $40 = 8 \times (\underline{\hspace{1cm}} + \underline{\hspace{1cm}})$

6. $(2 \times 8) + (\underline{\hspace{1cm}} \times 8) = 48$ $48 = 8 \times (\underline{\hspace{1cm}} + \underline{\hspace{1cm}})$

7. $(3 \times 8) + (\underline{\hspace{1cm}} \times 8) = 56$ $56 = 8 \times (\underline{\hspace{1cm}} + \underline{\hspace{1cm}})$

Write True or False in front of each statement. If the statement is false, explain why.

8. _____   Parallel lines do not intersect. _____

_____

9. _____   A triangle can have a pair of parallel sides. _____

_____

10. _____   A triangle is a quadrilateral. _____

_____

11. _____   A trapezoid is a quadrilateral. _____

_____

DAY 4

Solve mentally.

1. $4 \times 7 = $ _____   2. $64 \div 8 = $ _____   3. $56 \div 7 = $ _____

4. $3 \times 8 = $ _____   5. $49 \div 7 = $ _____   6. $63 \div 7 = $ _____

7. $4 \times 8 = $ _____   8. $24 \div 8 = $ _____   9. $48 \div 8 = $ _____

10. Kazuo is going to camp for 7 weeks. How many days will he be there? _____

11. If Kazuo goes to camp 3 days late and comes home
for one weekend, how many days will he be at camp? _____

DAY 5

Fill in the blanks. Look for a pattern.

1. $1 \times 10 =$ _____ $10 - 1 =$ _____

2. $2 \times 10 =$ _____ $20 - 2 =$ _____

3. $3 \times 10 =$ _____ $30 - 3 =$ _____

4. $4 \times 10 =$ _____ $40 - 4 =$ _____

5. $5 \times 10 =$ _____ $50 - 5 =$ _____

6. $6 \times 10 =$ _____ $60 - 6 =$ _____

7. What do you notice about the differences in problems 1 through 6? _____

_____

8. Write a rule for finding a multiple of 9 by first finding a multiple of 10. _____

_____

9. When Sarah plays hopscotch she can land on each square or she can jump over a single square. She always has to land with both feet on 4 and 5 and on 7 and 8. Tell three different ways Sarah can jump across the hopscotch board.

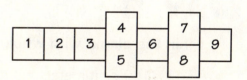

_____

DAY 6

Estimate. Don't write the sums. Draw a ring around the problems with sums less than 15,000.

1.	**2.**	**3.**	**4.**	**5.**
10,450	12,272	1002	1957	13,598
+ 1,553	+ 3,128	+ 899	+ 1957	+ 1,902

08   16   24   32   40   48   56   64   72   80

6. These numbers are consecutive multiples of 8. Find the sum of the digits in each

number. Describe the pattern you see. _____

_____

DAY 7

Fill in the blanks.

1. 6 feet = _____ yards

2. 7 feet = _____ yards

3. 8 feet = _____ yards

4. 9 feet = _____ yards

5. 10 feet = _____ yards

6. 11 feet = _____ yards

7. 12 feet = _____ yards

8. 14 feet = _____ yards

9. 19 feet = _____ yards

10. 23 feet = _____ yards

11. Ms. Sy takes the 7:56 A.M. train to work. She was late this morning and missed her train by 14 minutes. What time did she arrive at the train station? _____

12. Jake's plane was delayed 27 minutes. It finally took off at 8:25. What time was his plane originally scheduled to leave? _____

DAY 8

Fill in the blanks with whole numbers or decimal numbers.

1. 100 centimeters = _____ meter

2. 110 cm = _____ m

3. 200 cm = _____ m

4. 225 cm = _____ m

5. 300 cm = _____ m

6. 330 cm = _____ m

7. 400 cm = _____ m

8. 450 cm = _____ m

9. 500 cm = _____ m

10. 570 cm = _____ m

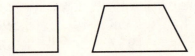

11. Describe two ways the figures are alike. _____

_____

12. Describe two ways the figures are different. _____

_____

_____

DAY 9

Problems 1 through 4 use the number 151,276.

1. Add 3 and round to the tens place. _____

2. Subtract 40 and round to the hundreds place. _____

3. Add 500 and round to the thousands place. _____

4. Add 3,000 and round to the ten thousands place. _____

5. Ellen bought eight packs of trading cards with three cards in each pack.
    Sam bought three packs of cards with six cards in each pack.
    Both paid the same amount. Who got the best deal? Explain.

_____

DAY 10   CHECKPOINT

Fill in the blanks with whole numbers, mixed numbers, or fractions.

1. 2 feet = _____ yard   2. 4 feet = _____ yards   3. 1 cup = _____ quart

4. 3 cups = _____ quart   5. 50 cm = _____ m   6. 25 cm = _____ m

7. 25 pennies = _____   8. 34 pennies = _____   9. 182 pennies = _____

Fill in the blanks.

10. $7 \times 3 =$ _____   11. $8 \times 3 =$ _____   12. $9 \times 3 =$ _____

    $7 \times 6 =$ _____ $8 \times 6 =$ _____ $9 \times 6 =$ _____

    $7 \times 9 =$ _____ $8 \times 9 =$ _____ $9 \times 9 =$ _____

Write True or False in front of each statement. If the statement is false, explain why.

13. _____   Parallel lines are always the same distance apart. _____

    _____

14. _____   A trapezoid has two pairs of parallel sides. _____

    _____

15. _____   All rectangles are squares. _____

    _____

DAY 11

Multiply mentally.

1. $2 \times 6 =$ _____

   $2 \times 60 =$ _____

   $20 \times 6 =$ _____

   $20 \times 60 =$ _____

   $2 \times 600 =$ _____

2. $7 \times 6 =$ _____

   $7 \times 60 =$ _____

   $70 \times 6 =$ _____

   $70 \times 60 =$ _____

   $7 \times 600 =$ _____

3. $7 \times 8 =$ _____

   $7 \times 80 =$ _____

   $70 \times 8 =$ _____

   $70 \times 80 =$ _____

   $7 \times 800 =$ _____

4. These are the first ten multiple of 9. Describe three patterns that you notice in this list. _____

_____

_____

09
18
27
36
45
54
63
72
81
90

DAY 12

Multiply mentally.

1. $3 \times 7 =$ _____

   $3 \times 70 =$ _____

   $30 \times 7 =$ _____

   $30 \times 70 =$ _____

   $3 \times 700 =$ _____

2. $8 \times 6 =$ _____

   $8 \times 60 =$ _____

   $80 \times 6 =$ _____

   $80 \times 60 =$ _____

   $8 \times 600 =$ _____

3. $8 \times 9 =$ _____

   $8 \times 90 =$ _____

   $80 \times 9 =$ _____

   $80 \times 90 =$ _____

   $8 \times 900 =$ _____

Draw a ring around the best measurement unit for each problem.

4. amount of water that fills a sink   cups   quarts

5. amount of soup in a serving   cups   quarts

6. length of a hair ribbon   feet   yards

7. length of a parking lot   feet   yards

8. weight of a strawberry   ounces   pounds

DAY 13

Solve mentally.

1.
```
   22
   22
   22
   22
   22
 + 22
```

2.
```
  132
 − 22

 − 22

 − 22

 − 22

 − 22

 − 22
```

3.
```
   22
 ×  6
```

4. $132 \div 6 =$

5. Describe one way a rhombus and a trapezoid are alike. _____

_____

6. Describe two ways a rhombus and a trapezoid are different. _____

_____

DAY 14

Fill in the remainder.

1. $49 \div 8 = 6$ R_____

2. $75 \div 8 = 9$ R_____

3. $67 \div 9 = 7$ R_____

4. $57 \div 7 = 8$ R_____

5. $49 \div 7 = 7$ R_____

6. $45 \div 9 = 5$ R_____

7. $83 \div 9 = 9$ R_____

8. $37 \div 9 = 4$ R_____

9. $57 \div 9 = 6$ R_____

10. The students in Mrs. Sharp's class bought ten times as many sports-booster buttons as the students in Mr. Wilson's class. The students in Mr. Wilson's class bought one gross or twelve dozen buttons. Write the number of buttons the students in Mrs. Sharp's class bought. Write it three different ways.

_____

DAY 15

Solve mentally.

1. $210 \div 3 =$ _____

2. $90 \times$ _____ $= 630$

3. $120 \div 20 =$ _____

4. $480 \div 6 =$ _____

5. _____ $\div 8 = 90$

6. $17 \times 20 =$ _____

7. $70 \times$ _____ $= 560$

8. $300 \div 5 =$ _____

9. $29 \times 10 =$ _____

10. $27 \times 10 =$ _____

11. $280 \div$ _____ $= 14$

12. $30 \times 20 =$ _____

13. If Alicia drives 60 miles per hour, how long will it take her to drive 200 miles?

_____

14. If she leaves home at 2 P.M. and wants to arrive at 7 P.M. will she make it on time? How do you know?

_____

_____

_____

DAY 16

Fill in the blanks.

1. $\frac{1}{4}$ quart $+ \frac{1}{2}$ quart $=$ _____ quart or _____ cups

2. $\frac{1}{8}$ quart $+ \frac{1}{2}$ quart $=$ _____ quart or _____ cups

3. $\frac{1}{4}$ quart $+ 1\frac{1}{2}$ quarts $=$ _____ quarts or _____ cups

Complete the patterns.

4. $\frac{1}{5}, \frac{2}{10}, \frac{3}{15}, \frac{4}{20},$ _____, $\frac{10}{50}$

5. $\frac{1}{8}, \frac{2}{16}, \frac{3}{24},$ _____, $\frac{8}{64}$

DAY 17

Fill in the blanks.

1. $\frac{1}{3}$ yard + $\frac{1}{3}$ yard = _____ yard or 2 feet

2. $\frac{1}{3}$ yard + $\frac{2}{3}$ yard = _____ yard or _____ feet

3. $\frac{1}{3}$ yard + $1\frac{1}{3}$ yards = _____ yards or _____ feet

4. $\frac{1}{3}$ yard + $\frac{1}{3}$ yard + 2 yards = _____ yards or _____ feet

5. Mr. Sanchez emptied his pockets and discovered that he had three twenty-dollar bills, five ten-dollar bills, six five-dollar bills, and four one-dollar bills. He also had two quarters, two dimes, one nickel, and three pennies. How much money did he have? _____

6. What are the fewest coins and bills Mr. Sanchez needs to make $150?

   _____

DAY 18

Fill in the blanks.

1. $\frac{3}{16}$ pound + $\frac{1}{4}$ pound = _____ pound or _____ ounces

2. $\frac{1}{2}$ pound + $\frac{3}{16}$ pound = _____ pound or _____ ounces

3. $\frac{1}{2}$ pound + $\frac{1}{2}$ pound = _____ pound or _____ ounces

4. 1 pound + $\frac{1}{16}$ pound = _____ pounds or _____ ounces

Write True or False in front of each statement. If the statement is false, explain why.

5. _____ All squares are parallelograms. _____

   _____

6. _____ All parallelograms are squares. _____

   _____

7. _____ All parallelograms have four right angles. _____

   _____

DAY 19

Fill in the blanks with whole numbers or decimals numbers.

1. 1000 milliliters = _____ liter

2. 500 milliliters = _____

3. 250 milliliters = _____

4. 100 milliliters = _____

5. 50 milliliters = _____

6. 2000 milliliters = _____

7. Hisoka has $\frac{1}{2}$ of his homework done. He can do $\frac{1}{8}$ more before the concert. How much homework will he still have to do when he comes home from the concert? _____

DAY 20

Problems 1 through 4 use the number 346,289.

1. Add 1 and round to the nearest ten. _____

2. Add 10 and round to the nearest hundred. _____

3. Add 800 and round to the nearest thousand. _____

4. Add 700,000, and round to the nearest ten thousand. _____

Solve this number riddle.

5. If you divide me by 1, my remainder is 0.
   If you divide me by 2, my reminder is 1.
   If you divide me by 3, my reminder is 2.
   If you divide me by 4, my reminder is 3.
   If you divide me by 5, my reminder is 3.
   If you divide me by 6, my reminder is 5.
   If you divide me by 7, my reminder is 2.
   I am less than 25. What number am I? _____

6. Now write your own number riddle. _____

   _____

   _____

MONTHLY ASSESSMENT

1. Name the shapes in the calendar pattern.

   _____

   _____

2. Write one name that includes all four shapes in the pattern.

   _____

3. Extend the shape pattern through April 30.

4. Put a check mark on each rhombus.

5. What is the pattern of the check marks?

   _____

   _____

6. Put an "X" on each rectangle that is not a square.

7. What is the pattern of the rectangles? _____

   _____

8. Make a pattern using different types of parallelograms. Describe your pattern using specific shape names.

   _____

   _____

9. Write three sentences about the patterns you see on your calendar.

   _____

   _____

   _____

   _____

   _____

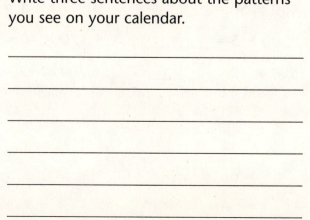

MONTHLY ASSESSMENT

Fill in the blanks.

1. 4 × 3 = _____
   ↓
   _____ × 3 = _____ and 4 × 9 = _____

2. 7 × 3 = _____
   ↓
   _____ × 3 = _____ and 7 × 9 = _____

3. (_____ × 8) + (2 × 8) = 48 and 48 = 8 × (_____ + 2)

4. 7 × 6 = _____   5. 8 × 7 = _____   6. 9 × 2 = _____

   7 × 3 = _____   8 × 5 = _____   9 × 4 = _____
   _____   _____   _____
   7 × _____ = 63   8 × _____ = 96   9 × _____ = 54

Solve mentally.

7. 4 × 7 = _____   8. 29 ÷ 7 = 4 R_____   9. 29 ÷ 4 = _____ R1

10. 9 × 10 = _____   11. 6 × _____ = 60   12. _____ × 10 = 30

    9 × 9 = _____   6 × 9 = _____   _____ × 9 = 27

13. 480 ÷ 6 = _____   14. 720 ÷ _____ = 90   15. _____ ÷ 20 = 7

Solve mentally.

16. 4 × 8 = _____   17.   5 × 5 = _____   18.   7 × 4 = _____

     4 × 80 = _____   5 × 50 = _____   7 × 40 = _____

     40 × 8 = _____   50 × 50 = _____   70 × 4 = _____

     40 × 80 = _____   500 × 5 = _____   70 × 40 = _____

     400 × 8 = _____   500 × 50 = _____   700 × 40 = _____

Fill in the blanks.

19. $\frac{3}{8}$ lb + $\frac{1}{2}$ lb = _____ lb or _____ oz

20. 1 lb + $\frac{1}{4}$ lb = _____ lb or _____ oz

21. $\frac{3}{16}$ lb + $\frac{1}{8}$ lb = _____ lb or _____ oz

MONTHLY ASSESSMENT

1   2   3   4   5   6   7   8   9

1. What is the sum of these numbers? _____

2. Write a sequence of nine consecutive numbers whose sum is 54.

   _____

3. Write a sequence of nine consecutive numbers whose sum is 72.

   _____

12 pencils

Case = 10 boxes of pencils

10 Cases of Pencils

4. How many pencils are in a case? _____

5. How many boxes are in ten cases? _____

6. How many pencils are in ten cases? _____

7. Describe one way to get exactly 276 pencils without taking any out of their boxes or cases.

   _____

8. If a box of pencils costs $1.20, what is the cost of one pencil? _____

9. What number am I?
   If you divide me by 1, my remainder is 0.
   If you divide me by 2, my reminder is 1.
   If you divide me by 3, my reminder is 2.
   If you divide me by 4, my reminder is 3.
   If you divide me by 5, my reminder is 2.
   If you divide me by 6, my reminder is 5.
   If you divide me by 7, my reminder is 5.
   I am between 25 and 50. What number am I? _____

10. There are five people in a room. Each person greets every other person with a handshake. How many handshakes will there be? _____

11. Describe how you got your answer. _____

    _____

MONTHLY ASSESSMENT

Fill in the blanks.

1 m	=	100 cm
1 yd	=	3 ft
1 qt	=	4 c
1 lb	=	16 oz

1. 1.5 m = _____ cm

2. $1\frac{1}{2}$ qt = _____ c

3. 14 c = _____ qt

4. 1 ft = _____ yd

5. 3 oz = _____ lb

6. 200 cm = _____ m

   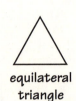 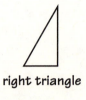

square   rhombus   parallelogram   trapezoid   equilateral triangle   right triangle

7. Place each figure in the correct part of this Venn Diagram or in the Extras list.

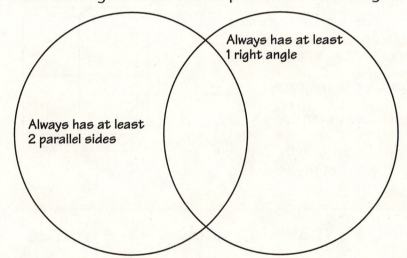

Extras

Always has at least 1 right angle

Always has at least 2 parallel sides

8. Place each figure in the correct part of this Venn Diagram or in the Extras list.

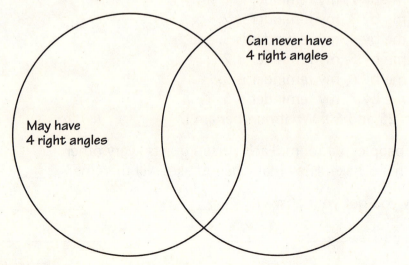

Extras

Can never have 4 right angles

May have 4 right angles

DAY 1

Fill in the blanks. Use each answer to find the next one.

1. $2 \times 2 = $ _____

   _____ $\times 2 = $ _____

   _____ $\times 2 = $ _____ and $16 \div 2 = $ _____

   _____ $\div 2 = $ _____

   _____ $\div 2 = 2$

2. $9 \times 2 = $ _____

   _____ $\times 2 = $ _____

   _____ $\times 2 = $ _____ and $72 \div 2 = $ _____

   _____ $\div 2 = $ _____

   _____ $\div 2 = $ _____

Complete the patterns.

3. 100, 95, 90, _____, 40.

4. 0, 5, 10, _____, 55.

DAY 2

Fill in the blanks. Use each answer to find the next one.

1. $2 \times 3 = $ _____

   _____ $\times 3 = $ _____ so $18 = 2 \times 3 \times $ _____

2. $5 \times 3 = $ _____

   _____ $\times 3 = $ _____ so $45 = $ _____ $\times 3 \times $ _____

3. $9 \times 3 = $ _____

   _____ $\times 3 = $ _____ so $81 = $ _____ $\times$ _____ $\times$ _____

4. Emily's plane leaves at 5:15 P.M. She needs 7 hours to get to the airport and get checked in. What time should she leave home? _____

DAY 3

Fill in the blanks.

1. $3 \times 4 = \underline{\hspace{1cm}}$ $3 \times 8 = \underline{\hspace{1cm}}$

2. $4 \times \underline{\hspace{1cm}} = 16$ $4 \times \underline{\hspace{1cm}} = 32$

3. $5 \times 4 = \underline{\hspace{1cm}}$ $5 \times 8 = \underline{\hspace{1cm}}$

4. $\underline{\hspace{1cm}} \times 4 = 24$ $6 \times 8 = \underline{\hspace{1cm}}$

5. $7 \times 4 = \underline{\hspace{1cm}}$ $\underline{\hspace{1cm}} \times 8 = 56$

6. $\underline{\hspace{1cm}} \times 4 = 32$ $8 \times 8 = \underline{\hspace{1cm}}$

7. $9 \times \underline{\hspace{1cm}} = 36$ $9 \times \underline{\hspace{1cm}} = 72$

 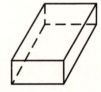

Cube   Rectangular Solid

8. Describe two ways the figures are alike. $\underline{\hspace{5cm}}$

$\underline{\hspace{12cm}}$

9. Describe two ways the figures are different. $\underline{\hspace{5cm}}$

$\underline{\hspace{12cm}}$

$\underline{\hspace{12cm}}$

DAY 4

Multiply mentally.

1. $2 \times 3 = \underline{\hspace{1cm}}$ $2 \times 6 = \underline{\hspace{1cm}}$

2. $3 \times 3 = \underline{\hspace{1cm}}$ $3 \times 6 = \underline{\hspace{1cm}}$

3. $4 \times 3 = \underline{\hspace{1cm}}$ $4 \times 6 = \underline{\hspace{1cm}}$

4. $5 \times 3 = \underline{\hspace{1cm}}$ $5 \times 6 = \underline{\hspace{1cm}}$

5. $6 \times 3 = \underline{\hspace{1cm}}$ $6 \times 6 = \underline{\hspace{1cm}}$

6. $7 \times 3 = \underline{\hspace{1cm}}$ $7 \times 6 = \underline{\hspace{1cm}}$

7. Ranie has three times the number of dolls that Isabel has. The number of dolls Ranie has is one less than the number of pennies in a quarter. How many dolls does Isabel have? $\underline{\hspace{1cm}}$

DAY 5

Fill in the blanks.

1. $1 \times 7 = \underline{\hspace{1cm}}$

2. $21 \div 3 = \underline{\hspace{1cm}}$

3. $28 \div 7 = \underline{\hspace{1cm}}$

4. $5 \times 7 = \underline{\hspace{1cm}}$

5. $7 \times 4 = \underline{\hspace{1cm}}$

6. $63 \div 7 = \underline{\hspace{1cm}}$

7. $42 \div 7 = \underline{\hspace{1cm}}$

8. $14 \div 2 = \underline{\hspace{1cm}}$

9. $3 \times 7 = \underline{\hspace{1cm}}$

10. $9 \times 7 = \underline{\hspace{1cm}}$

11. $56 \div 8 = \underline{\hspace{1cm}}$

12. $6 \times 7 = \underline{\hspace{1cm}}$

13. $10 \times 7 = \underline{\hspace{1cm}}$

14. $8 \times 7 = \underline{\hspace{1cm}}$

15. $63 \div 9 = \underline{\hspace{1cm}}$

16. Alisha has eight gumdrops and eight toothpicks. How many different three-dimensional shapes can she build? (It is not necessary to use all the gumdrops and toothpicks to create the shapes.) _____

17. What are the shapes she can build? _____

_____

_____

_____

DAY 6

Fill in the blanks.

1. $10 \times 6 = \underline{\hspace{1cm}}$

2. $70 \div 10 = \underline{\hspace{1cm}}$

3. $210 \div 30 = \underline{\hspace{1cm}}$

4. $240 \div 80 = \underline{\hspace{1cm}}$

5. $50 \times 50 = \underline{\hspace{1cm}}$

6. $270 \div 30 = \underline{\hspace{1cm}}$

7. $490 \div 70 = \underline{\hspace{1cm}}$

8. $560 \div 80 = \underline{\hspace{1cm}}$

9. $3000 \div 50 = \underline{\hspace{1cm}}$

10. $6300 \div 70 = \underline{\hspace{1cm}}$

11. $720 \div 80 = \underline{\hspace{1cm}}$

12. $810 \div 90 = \underline{\hspace{1cm}}$

13. Write a rule for a pattern of numbers that will have 5 and 3 as factors.

Show the first five numbers in your pattern. _____

_____

_____

_____

DAY 7

Subtract mentally.

1. 2000 − 456 = _____   2. 7525 − 75 = _____   3. 6503 − 106 = _____

4. 8223 − 225 = _____   5. 9733 − 166 = _____   6. 5453 − 249 = _____

7. Richie emptied his piggy bank. He had 15 quarters, 7 nickels, 11 dimes, and 23 pennies. How many whole dollars did he have? _____

8. How many extra cents did he have? _____

9. How much money did he have altogether? _____

DAY 8

Solve mentally.

1.	421 421 + 421	2.	421 × 3	3.	1325 1325 1325 1325 + 1325	4.	1325 × 5

5.	123 123 123 123 123 + 123	6.	123 × 6	7.	981 981 + 981	8.	981 × 3

9.	7002 7002 + 7002	10.	7002 × 3	11.	73,510 73,510 + 73,510	12.	73,510 × 3

13. Guess my shape.
    I am a three-dimensional shape. I can't roll.
    If I were real, you could put things in me.
    I have 6 identical faces. What shape am I? _____

DAY 9

Fill in the blanks. Use each answer to find the next one.

1. $7 \times 6 =$ _____
   _____ $\div 2 =$ _____
   _____ $\times 3 =$ _____
   _____ $\div 7 =$ _____
   _____ $\times 8 = 72$

2. $8 \times 7 =$ _____
   _____ $- 2 =$ _____
   _____ $\div 9 =$ _____
   _____ $\times 7 =$ _____
   _____ $\times 2 = 84$

3. Marcy got on the train at 7:30 A.M. and traveled 1 hour and 23 minutes to the next station. Samuel met her there. They boarded a train that left at 9:32 A.M. and arrived at 4:22 P.M. How many minutes did Marcy spend on a train that day? _____

DAY 10   CHECKPOINT

Next to the name of each solid, write the letters of the attributes that describe it.

SOLID	ATTRIBUTES
1. Cube _____	A. Has 12 edges
	B. Has 8 corners
2. Rectangular Solid _____	C. Has a point on the top
	D. Has at least one face that is a circle
3. Cylinder _____	E. Has 5 faces
	F. Has 6 faces
4. Sphere _____	G. Rolls
	H. Slides
5. Pyramid _____	I. Has at least one square face
	J. Has at least one triangular face
6. Cone _____	

Fill in the blanks. Use each answer to find the next one.

7. $3 \times 3 =$ _____
   _____ $\times 2 = 18$ so $18 = 3 \times 3 \times$ _____

DAY 11

Use the first and second answers to help you find the third.

1. $\begin{array}{r} 25 \\ \times\ 20 \\ \hline \end{array}$ $\begin{array}{r} 25 \\ \times\ 3 \\ \hline \end{array}$ $\begin{array}{r} 25 \\ \times\ 23 \\ \hline \end{array}$

2. $\begin{array}{r} 43 \\ \times\ 10 \\ \hline \end{array}$ $\begin{array}{r} 43 \\ \times\ 3 \\ \hline \end{array}$ $\begin{array}{r} 43 \\ \times\ 13 \\ \hline \end{array}$

3. $\begin{array}{r} 21 \\ \times\ 30 \\ \hline \end{array}$ $\begin{array}{r} 21 \\ \times\ 7 \\ \hline \end{array}$ $\begin{array}{r} 21 \\ \times\ 37 \\ \hline \end{array}$

Complete the patterns.

4. 104, 112, 120, 128, _____, 176.

5. 108, 99, 90, 81, _____, 0.

DAY 12

Fill in the blanks.

1. $150 \div 5 =$ _____ because _____ $\times\ 5 = 150$

2. $114 \div 2 =$ _____ because _____ $\times\ 2 = 114$

3. $66 \div 3 =$ _____ because _____ $\times\ 3 = 66$

4. $96 \div 4 =$ _____ because _____ $\times\ 4 = 96$

5. An airplane was scheduled to depart at 10:30 A.M. The plane was delayed $6\frac{1}{2}$ hours. What time did it leave? _____

6. An airplane coming from Atlanta is scheduled to arrive in Philadelphia at 3:35 P.M. This flight takes 2 hours and 15 minutes. What time did the plane leave Atlanta? _____

DAY 13

Draw a ring around the letter of the correct answer.

1. $\begin{array}{r} 93 \\ \times\, 3 \\ \hline \end{array}$ **A.** 279   **B.** 99   **C.** 276

2. $\begin{array}{r} 71 \\ \times\, 4 \\ \hline \end{array}$ **A.** 75   **B.** 285   **C.** 284

3. $\begin{array}{r} 67 \\ \times\, 2 \\ \hline \end{array}$ **A.** 144   **B.** 69   **C.** 134

cube   rectangular solid   cylinder

4. Describe two ways the solids are alike. _____
   _____

5. Describe two ways the cylinder differs from the cube and the rectangular solid.

   _____
   _____

DAY 14

Use the first answer to get the second.

1. 96 ÷ 4 = _____   98 ÷ 4 = 24 R _____

2. 96 ÷ 8 = _____   100 ÷ 8 = _____

3. 98 ÷ 7 = _____   99 ÷ 7 = _____

4. 126 ÷ 9 = _____   125 ÷ 9 = _____

5. This summer, Lila earns three times more money than
   Sarad earns. Sarad earns $125. How much does Lila earn? _____

DAY 15

Correct these wrong answers. Tell what you think the person who wrote the answers did wrong.

1.

$$\begin{array}{r} 200 \\ \times\ 20 \\ \hline 400 \end{array}$$

Correct answer: _____

_____

_____

2.

$$\begin{array}{r} 3000 \\ -\ 1765 \\ \hline 2765 \end{array}$$

Correct answer: _____

_____

_____

3. $750 \div 25 = 3$ Correct answer: _____

_____

_____

4. Theo has twelve toothpicks and eight gumdrops.
Each toothpick is a side. Each gumdrop is a vertex.
What three-dimensional shape can he make? _____

DAY 16

Fill in the blanks.

1. $\frac{1}{2}$ of \$0.50 + $\frac{1}{4}$ of \$1.00 = _____ cents.

2. $\frac{1}{4}$ quart + $\frac{1}{2}$ quart = _____ cups.

3. $\frac{1}{3}$ yard + $\frac{1}{3}$ yard = _____ feet.

Complete the pattern.

4. 0, 3, 7, 10, 14, 17, 21, _____, 45.

DAY 17

1. $\frac{1}{2}$ hour + $\frac{1}{4}$ hour = _____ minutes.

2. Tomas spent $\frac{1}{2}$ hour on homework and $\frac{1}{3}$ hour
   reading. How many minutes did he spend on both? _____

3. Seth drove $\frac{1}{4}$ hour. Then Garth took over driving.
   He drove the same length of time as Seth.
   How many minutes did they drive altogether? _____

4. Elizabeth lives $\frac{1}{3}$ hour from El Paso and Rosario lives $\frac{1}{4}$ hour from El Paso.
   How many more minutes will it take Elizabeth to get to El Paso than Rosario?

   _____

5. List five different ways to make $0.85. Do not use pennies. _____

   _____

DAY 18

1 oz $(\frac{1}{16}$lb$)$	1 oz $(\frac{1}{16}$lb$)$	1 oz $(\frac{1}{16}$lb$)$	1 oz $(\frac{1}{16}$lb$)$	1 oz $(\frac{1}{16}$lb$)$	1 oz $(\frac{1}{16}$lb$)$	1 oz $(\frac{1}{16}$lb$)$	1 oz $(\frac{1}{16}$lb$)$
1 oz $(\frac{1}{16}$lb$)$	1 oz $(\frac{1}{16}$lb$)$	1 oz $(\frac{1}{16}$lb$)$	1 oz $(\frac{1}{16}$lb$)$	1 oz $(\frac{1}{16}$lb$)$	1 oz $(\frac{1}{16}$lb$)$	1 oz $(\frac{1}{16}$lb$)$	1 oz $(\frac{1}{16}$lb$)$

1. $\frac{1}{4}$ lb + $\frac{1}{4}$ lb + $\frac{1}{4}$ lb = _____ lb or _____ oz

2. $\frac{1}{8}$ lb + $\frac{1}{8}$ lb + $\frac{1}{8}$ lb + $\frac{1}{8}$ lb + $\frac{1}{8}$ lb = _____ lb or _____ oz

3. $\frac{1}{16}$ lb + $\frac{1}{16}$ lb = _____ lb or _____ lb or _____ oz

What shape am I?

4. I am a three-sided, two-dimensional shape with two equal sides.

   I am _____

5. I am an eight-sided, two-dimensional shape.

   I am _____

6. I am a four-sided, two-dimensional shape with opposite sides

   equal and parallel. I am _____

7. I am a four-sided, two-dimensional shape with right angles

   and equal sides. I am _____

DAY 19

1 oz ($\frac{1}{16}$lb)	1 oz ($\frac{1}{16}$lb)	1 oz ($\frac{1}{16}$lb)	1 oz ($\frac{1}{16}$lb)	1 oz ($\frac{1}{16}$lb)	1 oz ($\frac{1}{16}$lb)	1 oz ($\frac{1}{16}$lb)	1 oz ($\frac{1}{16}$lb)
1 oz ($\frac{1}{16}$lb)	1 oz ($\frac{1}{16}$lb)	1 oz ($\frac{1}{16}$lb)	1 oz ($\frac{1}{16}$lb)	1 oz ($\frac{1}{16}$lb)	1 oz ($\frac{1}{16}$lb)	1 oz ($\frac{1}{16}$lb)	1 oz ($\frac{1}{16}$lb)

1. $\frac{1}{4}$ lb + $\frac{1}{2}$ lb = _____ lb or _____ oz

2. $\frac{1}{8}$ lb + $\frac{1}{8}$ lb + $\frac{3}{16}$ lb = $\frac{\quad}{16}$ lb or _____ oz

3. $\frac{1}{16}$ lb + $\frac{1}{16}$ lb + $\frac{1}{16}$ lb + $\frac{1}{16}$ lb + $\frac{3}{8}$ lb = $\frac{\quad}{16}$ lb or $\frac{\quad}{8}$ lb or _____ oz

4. $\frac{1}{16}$ lb + $\frac{1}{8}$ lb + $\frac{1}{4}$ lb + $\frac{1}{2}$ lb = $\frac{\quad}{16}$ lb or _____ oz

5. Callie got two times the number of A's as Liz. Liz got half as many as Stiles. Stiles got two A's during the year. How many A's did Liz get? _____

6. How many A's did Callie get? _____

DAY 20

Divide mentally.

1. 200 ÷ 20 = _____   2. 4200 ÷ 60 = _____   3. 4000 ÷ 200 = _____

4. 6300 ÷ 90 = _____   5. 2100 ÷ 300 = _____   6. 6400 ÷ 80 = _____

7. 3600 ÷ 90 = _____   8. 4900 ÷ 700 = _____   9. 3600 ÷ 600 = _____

10. 5600 ÷ 80 = _____   11. 3600 ÷ 4 = _____   12. 5600 ÷ 7 = _____

13. 8100 ÷ 90 = _____   14. 7200 ÷ 9 = _____

Corners	Parallel lines
Faces	
Right angles	*Edges*

Complete each definition using any or all of these words.

15. A rectangular solid has _____

_____

16. A trapezoid has _____

_____

17. A rhombus has _____

_____

1	2	3	4	5	6	7	8	9	10
11	12	13	14	15	16	17	18	19	20
21	22	23	24	25	26	27	28	29	30
31	32	33	34	35	36	37	38	39	40
41	42	43	44	45	46	47	48	49	50
51	52	53	54	55	56	57	58	59	60
61	62	63	64	65	66	67	68	69	70
71	72	73	74	75	76	77	78	79	80
81	82	83	84	85	86	87	88	89	90
91	92	93	94	95	96	97	98	99	100

1. Circle the multiples of 11 in the hundred chart.

2. Shade in the multiples of 12 in the hundred chart.

3. Write three things you notice about the patterns in your chart. _____

_____

_____

_____

MONTHLY ASSESSMENT

1. Write 36 as a product of 2's and 3's. _____

2. Explain why you can't write 42 as a product of 2's and 3's. _____

   _____

   _____

Fill in the blanks.

3. $2 \times 14 =$ _____ so _____ $\times 14 = 56$

4. $9 \times 3 =$ _____ so $9 \times$ _____ $= 54$

5. $10 \times 7 =$ _____

6. $220 \div 22 =$ _____

7. $3500 \div$ _____ $= 5$

8. $40 \times 40 =$ _____

9. $8100 \div$ _____ $= 90$

10. $70 \times$ _____ $= 7000$

11. $2000 - 15 =$ _____

12. $9733 - 833 =$ _____

13. $5450 - 249 =$ _____

Solve mentally.

14.
$$\begin{array}{r} 116 \\ 116 \\ 116 \\ + 116 \\ \hline \end{array}$$

15.
$$\begin{array}{r} 116 \\ \times 4 \\ \hline \end{array}$$

16.
$$\begin{array}{r} 1024 \\ 1024 \\ 1024 \\ 1024 \\ + 1024 \\ \hline \end{array}$$

17.
$$\begin{array}{r} 1024 \\ \times 5 \\ \hline \end{array}$$

Use the first two answers to help get the third.

18.
$$\begin{array}{r} 41 \\ \times 30 \\ \hline \end{array} \qquad \begin{array}{r} 41 \\ \times 5 \\ \hline \end{array} \qquad \begin{array}{r} 41 \\ \times 35 \\ \hline \end{array}$$

19.
$$\begin{array}{r} 106 \\ \times 20 \\ \hline \end{array} \qquad \begin{array}{r} 106 \\ \times 4 \\ \hline \end{array} \qquad \begin{array}{r} 106 \\ \times 24 \\ \hline \end{array}$$

Use the first answer to help get the second.

20. $25 \div 5 =$ _____

    $26 \div 5 =$ _____

21. $108 \div 9 =$ _____

    $107 \div 9 =$ _____

MONTHLY ASSESSMENT

Use the clock for these problems.

`6:45`

1. You have to be at the dentist's office at 8 A.M.
   It will take you $\frac{1}{2}$ hour to get there from home.
   How long will it be until you should leave home? _____

2. The snooze button lets you sleep ten more minutes. The alarm first
   went off at 6 A.M. and you're still in bed, waiting for the snooze alarm
   to wake you up. How many times have you pushed the snooze button? _____

3. How long until the snooze alarm rings again? _____

4. Your friend lives in a different time zone.
   At her house, it's three hours earlier than where
   you live. What time is it at your friend's house? _____

Solve each problem without using numbers in the problem to compute.
Explain how you solve each problem.

5. Mr. Jones earns $875 each week. He pays about $\frac{1}{3}$ of it in taxes. About how much

   does Mr. Jones pay in taxes each week? _____

   _____

6. Rafel runs $5\frac{1}{2}$ miles each day. Does he run at least 25 miles in a week? _____

   _____

7. May has 31 days in it. If you save $2.25 each day, will you have enough to buy a

   coat for $90 at the end of the month? _____

   _____

A	B	C	D	E	F	G	H	I	J	K	L	M	N	O	P	Q	R	S	T	U	V	W	X	Y	Z
1	2	3	4	5	6	7	8	9	10	11	12	13	14	15	16	17	18	19	20	21	22	23	24	25	26

Each letter of the alphabet is worth its number in alphabetical order.

8. How much is your name worth? _____

9. RAT and TAR are worth the same amount. You add an S to RAT. How can you give

   TAR an equal value? _____

   _____

Monthly assessment

Fill in the chart.

Name	Number of faces	Number of edges	Number of corners	Will it roll?	Will it slide?
1. Rectangular Solid					
2. Cube					
3. Cylinder					
4. Square Pyramid					
5. Cone					
6. Sphere					

Use these words to fill in the Venn Diagrams.

cylinder	cube	rectangle	triangle	sphere
rectangular solid	square	pyramid	circle	cone

7.

Can have some right angles

Can never have any right angles

Extras

8.

Is 3-Dimensional

Is 2-Dimensional

Extras